ELGAR

The Apostles

OPUS 49

an oratorio for soprano, alto, tenor
& three bass soli, SATB & orchestra

Order No: NOV 070097R

NOVELLO PUBLISHING LIMITED
8/9 Frith Street, London W1V 5TZ

NOTE.

The ancient Hebrew melody (Ps. xcii.) commencing on page 21 is quoted, by kind permission of the publishers, Messrs. Augener and Co., from the volume edited by Ernst Pauer, whose broad and appropriate harmony is retained in a few bars. Use is made of a portion of the Gregorian tone (freely adapted)—" Constitues eos"—the Gradual in which power is promised to the Apostles and their successors for all time. This theme, and other details concerning the music, will be found in the analysis.

E. E.

The sign *R* - - - -, signifies *ritardando.*
" " *A* - - - -, " *accelerando.*
" " *L* - - - -, " *largamente.*

A. M. D. G.

IN LONGDON MARSH
1902—3.

THE APOSTLES.

PROLOGUE.

CHORUS AND ORCHESTRA.

The Spirit of the Lord is upon me,
because He hath anointed me to preach the Gospel to the poor:
He hath sent me to heal the broken-hearted,
to preach deliverance to the captives
and recovering of sight to the blind,—
to preach the acceptable year of the Lord,

To give unto them that mourn a garland for ashes,
the oil of joy for mourning,
the garment of praise for the spirit of heaviness;
That they might be called trees of righteousness,
the planting of the Lord, that He might be glorified.

For as the earth bringeth forth her bud,
and as the garden causeth the things that are sown in it to spring forth;
So the Lord God will cause righteousness and praise to spring forth before all the nations.

The Spirit of the Lord is upon me,
because He hath anointed me to preach the Gospel.

PART I.

I.—THE CALLING OF THE APOSTLES.

RECIT. (TENOR).

And it came to pass in those days that Jesus went out into a mountain to pray, and continued all night in prayer to God.

(ORCHESTRA.)

The Angel Gabriel.

The voice of Thy watchman!
The Lord returneth to Zion,—
br k forth into joy,
sing together ye waste places of Jerusalem:
for the Lord hath comforted His people

(ORCHESTRA.)

The Angel.

"Behold My servant, Whom I have chosen;
My beloved, in Whom My soul is well pleased:
He shall not strive, nor cry aloud:
neither shall anyone hear His voice in the streets:
a bruised reed shall He not break,
the dimly burning wick shall He not quench,
and in His name shall the Gentiles hope."

The voice of Thy watchman!

THE DAWN.

SHOFAR (*distant*).

The Watchers (*on the Temple roof*).

It shines!

(*Clang of the Gates.*—SHOFAR.)

The face of all the East is now ablaze with light,
the Dawn reacheth even unto Hebron!

The Singers (*within the Temple*).

It is a good thing to give thanks unto the Lord,
and to sing praises unto Thy name, O Most High:

To shew forth Thy lovingkindness in the morning,
and Thy faithfulness every night,

Upon the psaltery;
upon the harp with a solemn sound.

For Thou, Lord, hast made me glad through Thy work:
I will triumph in the works of Thy hands.

For, lo, Thine enemies, O Lord. shall perish:
all the workers of iniquity shall be scattered.

The righteous shall flourish like the palm tree:
he shall grow like a cedar in Lebanon.

(SHOFAR AND ORCHESTRA.)

RECIT. (TENOR).

And when it was day, He called unto Him His disciples: and of them He chose twelve, whom also He named Apostles, that they should be with Him, and that He might send them forth to preach.

CHORUS.

The Lord hath chosen them
to stand before Him, to serve Him.
He hath chosen the weak to confound the mighty;
He will direct their work in truth.

Behold! God exalteth by His power,
who teacheth like Him?

The meek will He guide in judgment,
and the meek will He teach His way.
He will direct their work in truth,
for out of Zion shall go forth the law.

John, Peter, and Judas.

We are the servants of the Lord.

Peter.

Thou wilt shew us the path of life;
in Thy light shall we see light.
Let Thy work appear unto Thy servants.

John.

O blessed are they which love Thee,
for they shall rejoice in Thy peace:
and shall be filled with the law.

Judas.

We shall eat of the riches of the Gentiles,
and in their glory shall we boast ourselves.

John, Peter, and Judas.

For out of Zion shall go forth the law,
and the word of the Lord from Jerusalem.

CHORUS.

The Lord hath chosen them,
they shall be named the Priests of the Lord,
men shall call them the Ministers of our God.

John.

O blessed are they which love Thee.

Peter.

In Thy light shall we see light.

Judas.

God exalteth by His power.

CHORUS.

He will direct their work;
they are the servants of the Lord.

The Angel and CHORUS.

Thy watchmen shall lift up the voice;
with the voice together shall they sing:
for they shall see eye to eye,
when the Lord shall bring again Zion.

John, Peter, and Judas.

Come ye, and let us walk in the light of the Lord.

Jesus.

Behold, I send you forth.

He that receiveth you, receiveth Me;
and he that receiveth Me,
receiveth Him that sent Me.

John, Peter, and Judas.

We are the servants of the Lord.

The Angel.

Look down from heaven, O God,
and behold, and visit this vine.

CHORUS.

Amen.

II.—BY THE WAYSIDE.

Jesus.

BLESSED are the poor in spirit: for theirs is the kingdom of heaven.

Mary (The Blessed Virgin), John, and Peter.

(He setteth the poor on high from affliction:

Judas.

He poureth contempt upon princes.)

Jesus.

BLESSED are they that mourn: for they shall be comforted.

John.

(The Lord shall give them rest from their sorrow,

Peter.

and will turn their mourning into joy,

Mary and John.

and will comfort them:—

Women.

Weeping may endure for a night,

Men.

but joy cometh in the morning.)

Jesus.

BLESSED are the meek: for they shall inherit the earth.

The People.

(The meek also shall increase their joy—

Mary, John, and Peter.

in the Lord;

The People.

and the poor among men shall rejoice—

Mary, John, and Peter.

in the Holy One of Israel.)

Jesus.

BLESSED are they which do hunger and thirst after righteousness: for they shall be filled.

Mary, John, Peter, and Judas.

(Mercy and truth are met together:
righteousness and peace have kissed each other.

The People.

Sow to yourselves in righteousness,—)

Jesus.

BLESSED are the merciful: for they shall obtain mercy.

The People.

(Reap in mercy.

Mary, John, and Peter.

He that hath mercy on the poor, happy is he.

Judas.

The poor is hated even of his own neighbour:
the rich hath many friends.

The People.

Draw out thy soul to the hungry,

John.

and satisfy the afflicted soul;

Peter.

then shall thy light rise in obscurity.)

Jesus.

BLESSED are the pure in heart: for they shall see God.

Mary.

(Thou art of purer eyes than to behold evil.

John.

Blessed are the undefiled.

Peter.

Who can say, I have made my heart clean?

Judas.

The stars are not pure in his sight,

The People.

how much less man.)

Jesus.

BLESSED are the peacemakers: for they shall be called the children of God.

The People.

(The work of righteousness shall be peace.)

Jesus.

BLESSED are they which are persecuted for righteousness' sake: for theirs is the kingdom of heaven.

Rejoice, and be exceeding glad;
for great is your reward in heaven:
for so persecuted they the prophets which were before you.

SOLI AND CHORUS.

Blessed are they which have been sorrowful for all Thy scourges,
for they shall rejoice for Thee,
when they have seen all Thy glory,
and shall be glad for ever.

III.—BY THE SEA OF GALILEE.

RECIT. (TENOR).

And straightway Jesus constrained His disciples to get into a ship, and to go before Him unto the other side:
and He went up into a mountain to pray: and when the evening was come, He was there alone.
And His disciples went over the sea toward Capernaum.

IN THE TOWER OF MAGDALA.

Mary Magdalene.

O Lord Almighty, God of Israel, the soul in anguish, the troubled spirit, crieth unto Thee.
Hear and have mercy; for Thou art merciful: have pity upon me, because I have sinned before Thee.
Hear the voice of the forlorn, and deliver me out of my fear.
Help me, desolate woman, which have no helper but Thee:

Woe is me! for I am as when they have gathered the summer fruits—
as the grape-gleanings of the vintage.
Have pity upon me, because I have sinned before Thee.
My tears run down like a river day and night.

Whatsoever mine eyes desired I kept not from them, I withheld not my heart from any joy.

CHORUS (*Fantasy*).

Let us fill ourselves with costly wine and ointments,
and let no flower of the spring pass by us.
Let us crown ourselves with rosebuds before they be withered.

Mary Magdalene.

"Ye that kindle a fire, walk in the flame of your fire, and among the brands that ye have kindled.
This shall ye have of Mine hand; ye shall lie down in sorrow."

The mirth of tabrets ceaseth;
the noise of them that rejoice endeth,—
our dance is turned into mourning.

"This shall ye have of Mine hand; ye shall lie down in sorrow."

(*There arose a great tempest in the sea.*)

Mary Magdalene.

Is Thy wrath against the sea?

The voice of Thy thunder is in the heavens!
Deep calleth unto deep at the noise of Thy cataracts.

I see a ship in the midst of the sea, distressed with waves: and One cometh unto it, walking on the sea!.... and they that are in the ship, toiling in rowing, are troubled and cry out for fear.

The Apostles (in the ship).

It is a spirit!

Jesus.

Be of good cheer; It is I, be not afraid.

Peter.

Lord, if it be Thou, bid me come unto Thee upon the waters.

Jesus.

Come!

The Apostles.

He walketh on the waters,

Judas.

Fearfulness and trembling are come upon him, and an horrible dread hath overwhelmed him.

Peter.

Lord, save me; I perish!

Mary Magdalene.

He stretcheth forth His hand.

Jesus.

O thou of little faith; wherefore didst thou doubt?

Mary Magdalene.

The wind ceaseth, and they worship Him.

The Apostles.

Of a truth Thou art the Son of God.

Peter, John, and Judas.

The Lord hath his way in the whirlwind and in the storm.

Mary Magdalene.

Who stilleth the raging of the sea,—
Who maketh the storm a calm?

Thy providence, O Father, governeth it:
for Thou hast made a way in the sea,
and a safe path in the waves:
shewing that Thou canst save from all danger.

Thy face, Lord, will I seek.
Thou hast not forsaken them that seek Thee.
My soul followeth hard after Thee:
Thy right hand upholdeth me.

IN CÆSAREA PHILIPPI.

RECIT. (TENOR).

When Jesus came into the parts of Cæsarea Philippi, He asked His disciples, saying:

Jesus.

Whom do men say that I, the Son of man, am?

The Apostles.

Some say John the Baptist; some, Elias; and others, Jeremias, or one of the prophets.

Jesus.

But whom say ye that I am?

Peter.

Thou art the Christ, the Son of the living God.

Jesus.

Blessed art thou, Simon Bar-Jona: for flesh and blood hath not revealed it unto thee, but My Father Which is in heaven.
Thou art Peter,—
and upon this rock I will build My church; and the gates of hell shall not prevail against it.

SOLI AND CHORUS.

Proclaim unto them that dwell on the earth,
and unto every nation, and kindred, and tongue,
the everlasting Gospel.

Jesus.

And I will give unto thee the keys of the kingdom of heaven: and whatsoever thou shalt bind on earth shall be bound in heaven: and whatsoever thou shalt loose on earth shall be loosed in heaven.

IN CAPERNAUM.

Mary Magdalene.

Thy face, Lord, will I seek;
my soul followeth hard after Thee;
help me, desolate woman.

Mary.

Hearken, O daughter:—
When thou art in tribulation,
if thou turn to the Lord thy God,
and shall be obedient unto His voice,
He will not forsake thee.
Hearken, O daughter;—
Come thou, for there is peace to thee.

RECIT. (TENOR).

She stood at His feet weeping, and began to wash His feet with tears, and did wipe them with the hairs of her head, and kissed His feet, and anointed them with the ointment.

CHORUS (*Women*).

This man, if he were a prophet, would have known who and what manner of woman this is that toucheth him: for she is a sinner.

Mary Magdalene.

Hide not Thy face far from me:
put not Thy servant away in anger.

Jesus.

Thy sins are forgiven;
thy faith hath saved thee;—
Go in peace.

SOLI AND CHORUS.

Turn you to the stronghold, ye prisoners of hope.

To the Lord our God belong mercies and forgivenesses, though we have rebelled against Him;

Turn you to the stronghold, ye prisoners of hope.

The fear of the Lord is a crown of wisdom, making peace and perfect health to flourish;
both which are the gifts of God:
and it enlargeth their rejoicing that love Him.

Turn you to the stronghold, ye prisoners of hope.

Thou art a God of the afflicted,
Thou art an helper of the oppressed,
Thou art an upholder of the weak,
Thou art a protector of the forlorn,
A Saviour of them that are without hope.

Turn you to the stronghold, ye prisoners of hope.

Blessed is he who is not fallen from his hope in the Lord.
For He will forgive their iniquity, and He will remember their sin no more.

END OF PART I.

PART II.

IV.—THE BETRAYAL.

INTRODUCTION—(ORCHESTRA).

RECIT. (TENOR).

And it came to pass that He went throughout every city and village, preaching and shewing the glad tidings of the kingdom of God: and the Twelve were with Him;

And He began to teach them, that the Son of man must suffer many things, and be rejected, and be killed.

CHORUS.

"I will smite the Shepherd, and the sheep of the flock shall be scattered abroad."

Peter.

Be it far from Thee, Lord, this shall never be unto Thee.
Though all men shall be offended because of Thee, yet will I never be offended.

The Apostles.

Though we should die with Thee, yet will we not deny Thee.

CHORAL RECIT. (TENORS AND BASSES).

Then gathered the chief Priests and Pharisees a council, and said :—

" What do we ?
For this Man doeth many miracles."

So from that day forth they took counsel that they might put Him to death.

Then entered Satan into Judas, and he went his way, and communed with the chief Priests and Captains.

Judas.

What are ye willing to give me, and I will deliver Him unto you ?

CHORUS (TENORS AND BASSES).

And they weighed unto him thirty pieces of silver.
Judas then, having received a band of men and officers, cometh with lanterns and torches and weapons.

Judas.

Let Him make speed, and hasten His work, that we may see it; He shall bear the glory, and shall sit and rule upon His throne, the great King,—the Lord of the whole earth.)

Whomsoever I shall kiss, that same is He hold Him fast.

IN GETHSEMANE.

Judas.

Hail, Master!

Jesus.

Whom seek ye ?

The People.

Jesus of Nazareth.

Jesus.

I am He:
if therefore ye seek Me,
let these go their way.

RECIT. (CONTRALTO).

And they all forsook Him and fled;
but Peter followed Him afar off, to see the end.

CHORAL RECIT. (TENORS AND BASSES).

And they that had laid hands on Jesus, led Him away to the High Priest.

IN THE PALACE OF THE HIGH PRIEST.

Servants.

Thou also wast with Jesus of Nazareth;
this man was also with Him.

Peter.

I know not what thou sayest.

Servants.

Art not thou also one of His disciples ?

Peter.

As thy soul liveth, I am not.

Servants.

Did not we see thee in the garden with Him ?
Surely thou also art one of them.

Peter.

I swear by the Lord, I know not this Man of Whom ye speak.

RECIT. (CONTRALTO).

Then led they Jesus unto the hall of judgment.

CHORUS. (SOPRANOS AND CONTRALTOS).

And the Lord turned and looked upon Peter, and he went out, and wept bitterly.

RECIT. (CONTRALTO).

Then Judas, which had betrayed Him, when he saw that He was condemned, repented himself, and brought again the thirty pieces of silver to the chief Priests and Elders.

THE TEMPLE.

The Singers (*within the Temple*).

O Lord God, to Whom vengeance belongeth,
lift up Thyself, Thou Judge of the earth.

O Lord God, to Whom vengeance belongeth,
render a reward to the proud.

Lord, how long shall the wicked,
how long shall the wicked triumph?

Judas.

My punishment is greater than I can bear.

The Singers.

How long shall they utter and speak hard things?
and all the workers of iniquity boast themselves?

They break in pieces Thy people, O Lord,
and afflict Thine heritage.

Judas.

Mine iniquity is greater than can be forgiven.

The Priests.

A voice of trembling,—of fear,

Why art thou so grieved in thy mind?

Judas.

I have sinned in that I have betrayed the innocent blood.

The Priests.

What is that to us? See thou to that.

Judas.

I have sinned,—I have betrayed the innocent—

The Priests.

SELAH!

RECIT. (CONTRALTO).

And he cast down the pieces of silver and departed.

The Singers.

Lord, how long shall the wicked triumph?
Yet they say, The Lord shall not see;

He that planted the ear, shall He not hear?
He that formed the eye, shall He not see?

Judas (*without the Temple*).

Whither shall I go from Thy Spirit?
Or whither shall I flee from Thy presence?
If I say, Peradventure the darkness shall cover me,
then shall my night be turned to day;—
yea, the darkness is no darkness with Thee,
but the night is as clear as the day.

Sheol is naked before Thee,
and Abaddon hath no covering.

The Singers (*within the Temple*).

Blessed is the man whom Thou chastenest,
that Thou mayest give him rest from the days of adversity,—

Judas.

"Rest from the days of adversity,"—

Never man spake like this Man;
He satisfied the longing soul,
and filled the hungry soul with goodness.

The Singers.

—until the pit be digged for the wicked.

Judas.

Our life is short and tedious, and in the death of a man there is no remedy; neither was there any man known to have returned from the grave.
For we are born at all adventure, and we shall be hereafter as though we had never been; for the breath in our nostrils is as smoke, and a little spark in the moving of our heart,
which being extinguished, our body shall be turned into ashes, and our spirit shall vanish as the soft air,
and our name shall be forgotten in time, and no man have our work in remembrance; and our life shall pass away as the trace of a cloud, and shall be dispersed as a mist, that is driven away with the beams of the sun, and overcome with the heat thereof.

The Singers.

The Lord knoweth the thoughts of man,
that they are vanity.

Judas.

"The Lord knoweth the thoughts of man,"—

My hope is like dust that is blown away with the wind;
it is not possible to escape Thine hand,—
a sudden fear, and not looked for, comes upon me.

The People (*remote*).

Crucify Him!

Judas.

They gather themselves together and condemn the innocent blood.

The People.

Crucify Him!

Judas.

Mine end is come,—the measure of my covetousness;

over me is spread an heavy night, an image of that darkness which shall afterward receive me: yet am I unto myself more grievous than the darkness.

The Singers (within the Temple).

He shall bring upon them their own iniquity.

V.—GOLGOTHA.

"*Eli, Eli, lama sabachthani?*"

CHORUS.

Truly this was the Son of God.

Mary.

The sword hath pierced through mine own soul.

Mary and John.

Thou hast trodden the winepress alone,
and of Thy people there was none with Thee.
They shall look upon Him Whom they have pierced,
and they shall mourn for Him,
as one mourneth for his only son,
And shall be in bitterness for Him,
as one that is in bitterness for his firstborn.

Mary.

The sword hath pierced through mine own soul.

VI.—AT THE SEPULCHRE.

RECIT. (CONTRALTO).

And very early in the morning they came unto the sepulchre at the rising of the sun; and they entered in, and found not the body of the Lord Jesus.

The Watchers (on the Temple roof).

The face of all the East is now ablaze with light;
the Dawn reacheth even unto Hebron!

CHORUS (*Angels*) (SOPRANOS AND CONTRALTOS).

Alleluia!

Why seek ye the living among the dead?
He is not here, but is risen.
Behold the place where they laid Him.
Go, tell His disciples and Peter that He goeth before you into Galilee: there shall ye see Him, as He said unto you.

Alleluia!

VII.—THE ASCENSION.

The Apostles.

We trusted that it had been He which should have redeemed Israel.

Jesus.

Peace be unto you.

Behold, I send the promise of My Father upon you: but tarry ye in the city of Jerusalem, until ye be endued with power from on high.

The Apostles.

Lord, wilt Thou at this time restore again the kingdom to Israel?

Jesus.

It is not for you to know the times or the seasons, which the Father hath put in His own power.
But ye shall receive power, when the Holy Ghost is come upon you.
Go ye therefore, and teach all nations,
baptizing them in the name of the Father, and of the Son, and of the Holy Ghost;
and, lo, I am with you alway, even unto the end of the world.

RECIT. (CONTRALTO).

And when He had spoken these things—while He blessed them—He was taken up; and a cloud received Him out of their sight; and they looked stedfastly toward heaven.

The Apostles.

Give us one heart, and one way:
in Thy light shall we see light;
Thou wilt shew us the path of life.

MYSTIC CHORUS. (*In Heaven.*)

Alleluia!

Mary, Mary Magdalene, John, and Peter.

Give us one heart, and one way.

Mary.

My soul doth magnify the Lord:
and my spirit hath rejoiced in God my Saviour.

Mary Magdalene.

Thou drewest near in the day that I called upon Thee:
Thou saidst, Fear not.

Peter.

For He hath not despised nor abhorred the affliction of the afflicted;
neither hath He hid His face from him;

The Apostles and the Holy Women.

but when he cried unto Him, He heard.

MYSTIC CHORUS.

Alleluia!

"*Holy Father, keep through Thine own name those whom Thou hast given Me, that they may be one, as We are.*"

The Apostles and the Holy Women.

All the ends of the world shall remember and turn unto the Lord:
and all the kindreds of the nations shall worship before Thee.
for the kingdom is the Lord's:
and He is the Governor among the nations.

MYSTIC CHORUS.

Alleluia!

"*I have done Thy commandment.*
I have finished the work which Thou gavest Me to do;
I laid down My life for the sheep."

The Apostles.

"In the world ye shall have tribulation:
but be of good cheer:
I have overcome the world."

MYSTIC CHORUS.

"*What are these wounds in Thine hands?*"

"*Those with which I was wounded in the house of My friends.*"

They platted a crown of thorns,
and put it about His head,—
they mocked Him,—
they spat upon Him,—
they smote Him with a reed,—
they crucified Him.

Alleluia!

The Apostles and the Holy Women.

They shall come, and shall declare His righteousness
unto a people that shall be born, that He hath done this.

MYSTIC CHORUS.

"*Now I am no more in the world,*
but these are in the world,
and I come to Thee."

The Apostles and the Holy Women.

The kingdom is the Lord's:
and He is the Governor among the nations.

MYSTIC CHORUS.

From henceforth shall the Son of man be seated at the right hand of the power of God.

Mary, Mary Magdalene, John, and Peter.

In His love and in His pity He redeemed them.

Tutti.

Alleluia!

THE BLESSED VIRGIN } THE ANGEL }	... ...	*Soprano.*
MARY MAGDALENE	... ...	*Contralto.*
ST. JOHN	... ...	*Tenor.*
ST. PETER	... ...	*Bass.*
JUDAS	... ...	*Bass.*
JESUS	... ...	*Bass.*

CONTENTS.

PART I.

PROLOGUE.

		PAGE
CHORUS...	The Spirit of the Lord is upon me	1
	I.—THE CALLING OF THE APOSTLES.	
RECIT., TENOR	And it came to pass	12
	IN THE MOUNTAIN—NIGHT.	
ORCHESTRA	... ...	13
SOPRANO SOLO (*The Angel, Gabriel*)	The voice of Thy watchman	13
	THE DAWN.	
CHORUS, ALTO AND TENOR (*The Watchers on the Temple roof*) ...	It shines!	19
	MORNING PSALM.	
CHORUS	It is a good thing to give thanks unto the Lord... ...	21
RECIT., TENOR	And when it was day	27
{ CHORUS	The Lord hath chosen them	29
{ SOLI (*John, Peter and Judas*) ...	We are the servants of the Lord	42
{ SOLO (*The Angel*)	Thy watchmen shall lift up the voice	42
	II.—BY THE WAYSIDE.	
{ SOLO, QUASI RECIT. (*Jesus*)	Blessed are the poor in spirit	53
{ SOLI (*The Blessed Virgin, John, Peter and Judas*)	He setteth the poor on high from affliction	53
{ CHORUS	Weeping may endure for a night	55
	III.—BY THE SEA OF GALILEE.	
RECIT., TENOR	And straightway Jesus constrained His disciples ...	68
	IN THE TOWER OF MAGDALA.	
{ SOLO (*Mary Magdalene*)	O Lord Almighty, God of Israel	70
{ CHORUS (FANTASY)	Let us fill ourselves with costly wine	75
{ SOLO (*Mary Magdalene*)	Is Thy wrath against the sea?	85
{ SEMI-CHORUS (*The Apostles*) ...	It is a Spirit	88
{ SOLO (*Jesus*)	Be of good cheer	89
{ SOLO (*Peter*)	Lord, if it be Thou, bid me come unto Thee	89
	IN CÆSAREA PHILIPPI.	
RECIT., TENOR	When Jesus came into the parts of Cæsarea Philippi ...	97
RECIT. (*Jesus*)	Whom do men say that I, the Son of man, am? ...	97
CHORUS	Some say, John the Baptist	98
SOLO (*Peter*)	Thou art the Christ	98
SOLO (*Jesus*)	Blessed art thou, Simon Bar-Jona	100
SOLI AND CHORUS	Proclaim unto them that dwell on the earth	100
SOLO (*Jesus*)	And I will give unto thee the keys of the Kingdom of Heaven	102
SOLO (*Mary*)	Hearken, O daughter	103
RECIT., TENOR	She stood at His feet weeping	104
CHORUS (*Women*)	This man, if He were a prophet	105
SOLO (*Mary Magdalene*)	Hide not Thy face far from me	107
SOLO (*Jesus*)	Thy sins are forgiven	108
SOLI AND CHORUS	Turn you to the stronghold, ye prisoners of hope ...	109

PART II.

		PAGE
INTRODUCTION (ORCHESTRA)		126

IV.—THE BETRAYAL.

RECIT., TENOR	And it came to pass	128
CHORUS	I will smite the Shepherd	129
SOLO (*Peter*)	Be it far from Thee, Lord	130
CHORUS (*The Apostles*)	Though we should die with Thee	130
CHORUS, TENOR AND BASS	Then gathered the chief Priests and Pharisees	131
SOLO (*Judas*)	What are ye willing to give me?	133
CHORUS, TENOR AND BASS	And they weighed unto him thirty pieces of silver	134
SOLO (*Judas*)	Let Him make speed, and hasten His work	136

IN GETHSEMANE.

SOLO (*Judas*)	Hail, Master	138
SOLO (*Jesus*)	Whom seek ye?	138
CHORUS	Jesus of Nazareth	138
SOLO (*Jesus*)	I am He	139
RECIT., CONTRALTO	And they all forsook Him	139
CHORUS	And the Lord turned and looked upon Peter	144

THE TEMPLE.

RECIT., CONTRALTO	And Judas, which had betrayed Him	145
CHORUS	O Lord God, to whom vengeance belongeth	146
SOLO (*Judas*)	My punishment is greater than I can bear	147

WITHOUT THE TEMPLE.

SOLO (*Judas*)	Whither shall I go from Thy Spirit?	153
CHORUS	Blessed is the man whom Thou chastenest	154

V.—GOLGOTHA.

ORCHESTRA	"*Eli, Eli, lama sabachthani?*"	166
CHORUS	Truly, this was the Son of God	166
SOLO (*Mary*)	The sword hath pierced through mine own soul	166
SOLO (*John*)	Thou hast trodden the wine press alone	167

VI.—AT THE SEPULCHRE.

RECIT., CONTRALTO	And very early in the morning	169
CHORUS (*The Watchers*)	The face of all the East	169
SEMI-CHORUS, SOPRANO & CONTRALTO	Why seek ye the living?	172

VII.—THE ASCENSION.

CHORUS (*The Apostles*)	We trusted that it had been He	176
SOLO (*Jesus*)	Peace be unto you	177
CHORUS (*The Apostles*)	Lord, wilt Thou at this time restore	178
SOLO (*Jesus*)	It is not for you to know the time or the seasons	178
RECIT., CONTRALTO	And when He had spoken these things	181

IN HEAVEN.

SEMI-CHORUS AND CHORUS	Alleluia!	182

ON EARTH.

SOLI AND CHORUS	Give us one heart and one way	182

THE APOSTLES.

PROLOGUE.

Edward Elgar, Op. 49.

2
Soprano.
pp
The Spir-it of the Lord is up - on me, be-
Alto.
pp
The Spir-it of the Lord is up - on me, be-
CHORUS.
Tenor.
pp
The Spir-it of the Lord is up - on me, be-
Bass.
pp
The Spir-it of the Lord is up - on me, be-
2
-cause He hath a - noint - ed me to preach the
cresc.
-cause He hath a - noint - ed me to preach the
cresc.
-cause He hath a - noint - ed me to preach the
cresc.
-cause He hath a - noint - ed me to preach the
cresc.
espress.
3
3

3
p
pp espress.
Gos - pel to the poor: He hath sent me to heal the
Gos - pel to the poor: He hath sent me to heal the broken-
Gos - pel to the poor: He hath sent me to heal the broken-
Gos - pel to the poor: He hath sent me to heal the
largamente
dim.
bro-ken-hearted, to preach de-liv'rance to the cap-tives and re-
- heart - ed, to preach de-liv'rance to the cap-tives and re-
- heart - ed, to preach de-liv'rance to the cap-tives
bro-ken-hearted, to preach de-liv'rance to the cap-tives
pp dolce
pp

cresc. molto
cov'r - - - ing of sight to the
cov'r - - - ing of sight to the
and re - cov'r - ing of sight to the
and re - - cover - ing of sight to the
f
Ped.
Ped.
4
L
ff
sf
blind, — to preach the acceptable year of the Lord; —
blind, — to preach the acceptable year of the Lord; —
blind, — to preach the acceptable year of the Lord; —
blind, — to preach the acceptable year of the Lord; —
Ped.
Ped.

poco animato
5 dolce e legato

pp

To give un-to them that

pp dolce e legato

To give un-to them that

ff R.H. L.H. R.H. L.H. dim.
sonore e largamente
Ped.

5 dolce e legato
pp poco animato
con Ped.

pp poco

mourn a garland for ash- - es, the oil of joy for mourning, the

pp poco

mourn a garland for ash- - es, the oil of joy for mourning, the

gar-ment of praise for the spir-it of heav-i-ness; That
gar-ment of praise for the spir-it of heav-i-ness; That
poco rall.
they might be call - - ed trees of right-eousness,
poco rall.
they might be call - - ed trees of right-eousness,
poco rall.

6 tranquillo
pp
the planting of the Lord, that He might be glo - ri - fied.
pp
the planting of the Lord, that He might be glo - ri - fied.
pp
the planting of the Lord, that He might be glo - ri - fied.
pp
the planting of the Lord, that He might be glo - ri - fied.
6
pp tranquillo
7 poco rit.
p dolce
For
pp
For as the earth bringeth forth her
poco rit.
pp
For as the earth bringeth forth her
7 poco rit.
ppp

Più mosso.
legato
as the earth, the earth bringeth forth her bud, and as the
bud,
bud,
Più mosso. ♩ = 80.
pp
dim.
gar - den caus - eth the things that are sown in it to
dim.

dolce
8
f sostenuto
spring forth; So the Lord God will cause right-
So the Lord God will cause right-
So the Lord God will cause right-
So the Lord God will cause right-
ten.
Ped.
con Ped.
ff
-eousness and praise to spring forth be-fore all the
-eousness and praise to spring forth be-fore all the
-eousness and praise to spring forth be-fore all the
-eousness and praise to spring forth be-fore all the
ten.

dim.
p
poco rit.
na - tions. As the earth bringeth forth her
na - tions. As the earth bringeth forth her
na - tions. As the earth, the earth bring-eth forth her
na - tions. As the earth, as the earth bringeth forthher
dim.
p
poco rit.
9
a tempo
Tempo I°
bud.
bud.
bud.
bud.
a tempo
poco a poco ritardando al - - Tempo I°
pp
3
3

ppp
10
The Spir-it of the Lord is up - on me, — because He hath a -
The Spir-it of the Lord is up - on me, — because He hath a -
The Spir-it of the Lord is up - on me, — because He hath a -
The Spir-it of the Lord is up - on me, — because He hath a -
11
dim.
- noint - ed me to preach the Gos-pel. ———
- noint - ed me to preach the Gos-pel. ———
- noint - ed me to preach the Gos-pel. ———
- noint - ed me to preach the Gos-pel. ———
pp
dim.

I.

THE CALLING OF THE APOSTLES.

IN THE MOUNTAIN, — NIGHT.

17
dim.
mf
of thy watchman!
The
poco accel.
pp
ppp
pp
p
♩= 69.
f
stringendo
animato
f
Lord
re - turn - eth
to
Zi - on:—
break
fp
stringendo
forth in - to joy,
sing
to - geth-er
ye
dim.
rit.
18
tranquillo. ♩= 60.
molto rit.
p
waste
pla-ces
of Je-ru-sa-lem:
for the Lord
hath
dim.
rit.

pp
com - forted His peo-ple.
a tempo ♩=56.
colla parte
rit.
ppp
19 ♩=50.
pp
ppp allargando
molto stringendo
f
mf
sonore
pp
ppp
a tempo ♩=50.
nobilmente.
3
rit.
a tempo ♩=50.
molto tranquillo.
ppp
Ped.
20
THE ANGEL.
p
"Be-hold My
Più mosso. ♩=60.
pp

animato
ser - - vant, Whom I have cho - - sen; My be -
- lov - - - - ed, in Whom My soul is well
L.H.
L.H.
R.H.
21
tranquillo espress.
pleas - ed:
He shall not
molto espress.
strive, nor cry a - loud: neither shall a - ny-one

hear His voice in the streets:
Ped.
22
p dolcissimo
pp
a bruis - ed reed shall He not break, the dim - ly burn - ing
pp
cresc. allargando dim.
wick shall He not quench, and in His name shall the
allargando
Ped. ✻Ped. ✻
a tempo
Gen-tiles hope."
a tempo
fp

C

23
fp
ppp
pp
The voice of thy
watch - man!
24
a tempo ♩ = 50.
rit.
ppp
allargando
a tempo
sonore

THE DAWN.

STAND
25 Allegro moderato.
Alto.
CHORUS.
Tenor.
THE WATCHERS,
(on the Temple roof)
p
It shines!
p
It shines!
25 Allegro moderato. ♩ = 88.
SHOFAR (distant)
pp Clar.
Strings.
4 Horns.
p
animato
mf
p
p
(♩ = 96.)
f
p
f
26
p Shofar.
a tempo
f
ff
Strings.

Alto.
27 Maestoso. molto marcato
The face of all the East
Tenor.
The face of all the East
27 Maestoso. ♩= 80.
sf pp molto cresc.
is now a - blaze with light, the
is now a - blaze with light, the
Ped.
allargando
ff
28 a tempo
Dawn reach-eth e-ven un-to He - bron!
Dawn reach-eth e-ven un-to He - bron!
28 Maestoso. ♩=72.
p allargando
cresc.
ff

MORNING PSALM.
(within the Temple)

* Ancient Hebrew melody, Psalm XCII.

cresc. allargando
a tempo
morn-ing, and Thy faith-ful-ness ev' - - ry night,
cresc. allargando
a tempo
morn-ing, and Thy faith-ful-ness ev' - - ry night,
cresc. allargando
a tempo
and Thy faith-ful-ness ev' - - ry night,
cresc. allargando
a tempo
and Thy faith-ful-ness ev' - - ry night,
a tempo
allargando
dim.
p cantabile
dolce
Up - on the psal - tery; up - on the harp
p cantabile
dolce
Up - on the psal - - tery; up - on the harp
p cantabile
dolce
Up - on the psal - tery; up - on the harp

pp
with a sol-emn sound.
pp
with a sol-emn sound.
pp
with a sol-emn sound.
p cresc.
For Thou, Lord, hast made me glad thro' Thy
p cresc.
For Thou, Lord, hast made me glad thro' Thy
cresc.
molto allargando
30
a tempo
f
ff
p
I will triumph in the works of Thy hands. For,
I will triumph in the works of Thy hands. For,
work: I will triumph in the works of Thy hands. For,
work: I will triumph in the works of Thy hands. For,
sf
f
ff molto allargando
a tempo
dim.
p

dim.
lo, Thine en-e-mies, O Lord, shall per-ish; all the workers of in-
lo, Thine en-e-mies, O Lord, shall per-ish; all the workers of in-
lo, Thine en-e-mies, O Lord, shall per-ish; all the workers of in-
lo, Thine en-e-mies, O Lord, shall per-ish; all the workers of in-
dim.
-i-qui-ty shall be scat-tered. The righteous shall flourish like the
-i-qui-ty shall be scat-tered. The righteous shall flourish like the
-i-qui-ty shall be scat-tered.
-i-qui-ty shall be scat-tered.

31
pp
dim.
palm tree: he shall grow like a ce - dar in Le - ba - non.
palm tree: he shall grow like a ce - dar in Le - ba - non.
he shall grow like a ce - dar in Le - ba - non.
he shall grow like a ce - dar in Le - ba - non.
Shofar.
L.H.
32
animato poco a poco
pp
Allegro moderato. ♩ = 96.
dolce

33
cresc. - poco
- a -
poco
ff
sempre cresc. ed animato
Shofar
34
♩ = 104.
sf
Ped.
sempre ff
rall. -
ff

35 *Più lento.* ♩ = 80.

8

fffz *solenne*

con Ped.

fffz *rall.*

ppp *rall. molto*

8va bassa

36 Tenor. Recit. *ad lib.*

f *p dolce*

And when it was day, He call - ed un - to Him His dis -

pp colla parte (♩ = 84)

a tempo *allargando* *cresc. e marcato*

- ci - ples; and of them He chose twelve ___ whom

espress. *a tempo* *ten.* *Più lento.* *pp allargando*

3

37
a tempo
p dolce
al-so He nam-ed A-pos- - - - - - tles; that
a tempo
colla parte
dolce
Ped.
they should be with Him; and that He might
pp
f
38
largamente
a tempo
send them forth to preach.
f
colla parte
cresc.
animato
R.H
sf
sf
sf
sf

CHORUS.

39 Allegro.
Soprano.
Alto.
Tenor.
Bass.
maestoso.
f
The Lord hath cho-sen them to
stand be - fore Him to serve Him.
Allegro. ♩=108.
ff
Ped.
cresc.
animato
mf
ff animato
8ves

40
He hath cho - sen the weak to con-found the
He hath
He hath cho - sen the weak,
He hath cho - sen
40 = 116.
cresc.
might - y, He hath cho - sen the weak to con-found the
cho - sen the weak, He hath
He hath cho - sen the weak,
the weak to con - found the might - y, He hath cho -

animato
mighty; He will di-rect their work in
cho - sen the weak to con-found the might-y;
He will di-rect their work in
- - sen the weak to con-found the mighty.
animato
41
truth Be-hold! God ex-
Be-hold! God ex-alt-eth
truth. Be-hold! God ex-
Be-hold! God ex-alt-eth
41 ♩= 126.

42
sf
p
-alt-eth by His pow'r; who teacheth like
by His pow'r; who teacheth like
-alt-eth by His pow'r; who
by His pow'r; who
42 dolce
sf
p
Ped.
Ped.
Ped.
pp legato
Him? The meek will He guide in judg - ment,
Him? The meek will He guide in judg - ment,
teacheth like Him? The meek will He guide in judg - ment,
teacheth like Him? The meek will He guide in judg - ment,
dim.
Ped.

43

poco rit.

— and the meek will He teach His way. He will di -

— and the meek will He teach — His way.

— and the meek will He teach His way.

— and the meek will He teach His way.

43 *poco rit.*

dolce

Ped. *

JOHN. *mf* *poco allargando*

We are the ser-vants of the

PETER. *mf* *poco allargando*

We are the ser-vants of the

JUDAS. *mf* *poco allargando*

We are the ser-vants of the

poco allargando

-rect their work in truth,

p *poco allargando*

He will di - rect their work in truth,

p

He will — di-rect their work, He will di - rect their

p

He will di - rect their work in truth, He will di - rect their

p

poco allargando

44 Tempo I°
poco largamente
dim.
Lord.
dim.
f espress.
Lord.
Thou wilt shew us the
dim.
Lord.
44 Tempo I°
poco largamente
pp
He will di - rect their work in truth.
pp
He will di - rect their work in truth.
pp
work, He will di-rect their work in truth.
pp
work, He will di-rect their work in truth.
44 Tempo I° ♩=96.
pp
p poco largamente
PETER.
path of life; in Thy light shall
we see light. Let Thy work ap
f

ten.

45

\- pear ___ un - to Thy ser - vants.

CHORUS.

pp He hath cho - sen

pp He hath

45

pp

PETER.

mf In ___ Thy light shall we see

JUDAS.

mf In ___ Thy light shall we see

pp He hath cho-sen them.

them to confound the mighty.

pp He hath cho-sen them to stand be-fore Him.

cho - sen them, He hath cho-sen them to stand be-fore Him.

46 JOHN.
f
O bless - ed are they which love
light.
light.
46
p
Thee, for they shall re - joice in Thy peace:
f deciso.
We shall eat of the
ten.
and shall be fill - - ed with the
mf
In Thy light shall we see
sf
rich - es of the Gen - tiles, and in their glo - ry shall we
marcato

47
dim.
law.
dim.
light.
boast ourselves.
47
p
cresc.
He hath cho-sen the weak to con-found the
mf
He hath
p
cresc.
He hath cho - sen the weak,
mf
He hath cho - sen
CHORUS.
47
cresc.
mf
dim.
might - y, He hath cho - sen the weak to con-found the
p
cho - sen the weak, to con-found the
mf
dim.
He hath cho - sen the weak.
dim.
the weak to con - found the might - y to con-found the
mf
dim.

48
JOHN.
p
cresc.
For out of Zi - on shall go forth the
might - y. Out of Zi - on shall
might - y. Out of Zi - on shall
Out of Zi - on shall
might - y. Out of Zi - on shall
pp
48
cresc.
law, and the word of the Lord from Je -
PETER.
and the word, the word of the Lord from Je - ru -
JUDAS.
and the word of the Lord from Je - ru -
go forth the law.
go forth the law.
go forth the law.
go forth the law.
f

A
-ru-sa-lem.
- - sa-lem.
- - sa-lem.
ff
The
ff
The
ff
The
ff
The
A
ff
R.H.
sf
Ped.
sf
Ped.
sf
Ped.
Ped.
10
49
tempo
andioso.
Lord, the Lord hath cho - sen them, they shall be
Lord, the Lord hath cho - sen them, they shall be
Lord, the Lord hath cho - sen them, they shall be
Lord, the Lord hath cho - sen them, they shall be
3
49
a tempo ♩=116.
ff Grandioso.
con Ped. non legato

animato
rf
named the Priests of the Lord,
men shall call them the
men shall call them the
men shall call them
animato
Ped.
ten.
Min - is - ters, men shall call them the Min-is-ters of our
𝅗𝅥 = 72.

50
JOHN.
mf espress.
O blessed are they which love Thee.
PETER.
mf
In Thy light shall we see light.
JUDAS.
mf
God exalteth by His power.
50
God.
p
God.
p
God.
p
f
They are the servants of the
God.
p
f
They are the servants of the
50
p
poco allargando
51
mf
For out of Zion shall go forth the
mf
For out of Zion shall go forth the
mf
For out of Zion shall go forth the
mf
He will direct their work.
51
pp dim.
mf
pp dim.
He will direct their work in truth.
p
pp
Lord.
He hath chosen
p
pp
Lord.
He hath chosen
51
pp colla parte

THE ANGEL.
p
Thy watch - men shall lift
Poco più mosso.
dim.
law.
dim.
law.
dim.
law.
Soprano I.
p pp
Thy watch - men shall lift up the voice;
Soprano II.
p pp
Thy watch - men shall lift up the voice;
Contralto I.
p pp
Thy watch - men shall lift up the voice;
Contralto II.
p pp
Thy watch - men shall lift up the voice;
Tenor.
them.
Bass.
them.
Poco più mosso. 𝅗𝅥 = 80.

cresc. e stringendo
up the voice; with the voice to - geth - er
Soprano I.
with the voice together shall they sing,
Soprano II.
with the voice together shall they sing,
Contralto I.
with the voice together shall they sing,
Contralto II.
with the voice together shall they sing,
cresc. e stringendo
f
shall they sing:
52
a tempo
for they shall
mf
dim.
pp
shall they sing:
shall they sing:
shall they sing:
shall they sing:
52 a tempo 𝅗𝅥 = 84.
dim.
pp

see, shall see eye to eye,
Soprano.
They shall
Alto.
Tenor.
Bass.
when the Lord shall bring a - gain
see, shall see eye to eye, when the
They shall see eye to eye, when the
When the

Zi - on.
pp
dim.
Lord, when the Lord shall bring a-gain
dim.
Lord, when the Lord, the Lord shall bring a-gain
dim.
Lord, the Lord shall bring, shall bring a-gain
p
dim.
When the Lord shall bring a-gain
ten.
espress.
dim.
53 THE ANGEL.
p
They
JOHN.
p
Come ye, let us walk in the light of the
PETER.
pp
Come ye, let us walk in the light of the
JUDAS.
pp
Come ye, let us walk in the light of the
53
pp
Zi-on.
pp
They shall be
pp
Zi-on.
pp
They shall be
pp
Zi-on.
pp
They shall be
pp
Zi - on.
They shall be
53
pp

dolce
lift up the voice, — for they shall see eye to
p
Lord. In Thy light shall we see
p
Lord. In Thy light shall we see
p
Lord. In Thy light shall we see
named the Priests of the Lord, ——— of the Lord.
named the Priests, shall be nam-ed the Priests of the Lord.
named the Priests of the Lord, shall be named the Priests of the
named the Priests of the Lord.

54
dolce
eye,
when the Lord
light.
light.
light.
54
pp
The meek will He teach His
pp
Lord.
The meek will He teach His
molto cresc.
He will di - rect their work in truth.
(𝅗𝅥 = 96).
54

shall bring again Zi - on.
For out of Zi - on
For out of Zi - on
Out of Zi - on
way, they shall be nam - ed the Priests
He will di - rect their work in truth. He
way, will He teach His way.
The meek will He guide. He

JESUS.
55
espress.
f
Be - hold, I send you
dim. molto
ppp
shall go forth the law.
dim. molto
ppp
shall go forth the law.
dim. molto
ppp
shall go forth the law.
55
ppp
— of the Lord, — Men shall call them the
3
ppp
3
— will di - rect their work, Men — shall call — them the
ppp
3
Men — shall call — them the
3
ppp
— will di - rect their work, Men shall call them the
55 o = 60.
3
dim.

forth, He that re - ceiv - eth you, re - ceiv - eth
Min-is-ters of our God.
Min-is-ters of our God.
Min-is-ters of our God.
Min-is-ters of our God.
ppp
con Ped.
56
Me, and he that re - ceiv - eth Me, re -
pp
God hath cho - sen them.
God hath cho - sen them.
God hath cho - sen them.
God hath cho - sen them.
56
mf

tranquillo
-ceiv-eth Him that sent Me.
ppp
The Spir-it of the Lord is up-on Him.
The Spir-it of the Lord is up-on Him.
The Spir-it of the Lord is up-on Him,
The Spir-it of the Lord is up-on Him,
tranquillo
ppp
THE ANGEL.
57
pp
Look down from heaven, O
JOHN.
pp
We are the servants of the Lord.
PETER.
pp
We are the servants of the Lord.
JUDAS.
pp
We are the servants of the Lord.
57
the Spir-it
the Spir-it
57

58
pp
God,
and be-hold,
dim. molto
of the Lord is up-on Him,
dim. molto
of the Lord is up-on Him,
58
and vis-it this vine.
R
59 Lento.
pp
A-men.
A-men.
A-men.
A-men.
R
Lento. 𝅗𝅥 = 72.
allargando
59
solenne
SIT
ff
fff
dim. subito
p
Ped

II.

BY THE WAYSIDE.

dim.
high from af - flic - tion.
- flic - - tion.
high.
parlando
p
He pour - eth con - tempt up - on prin - ces.
p
pp
61
JESUS. Recit. espress.
A
poco cresc.
R
dim.
p
Blessed are they that mourn; for they shall be com-fort - ed.
Andante.
colla parte
quasi Allegretto.
JOHN. dolce
p
The Lord shall give them rest from their sor - row,
PETER.
p
And will
quasi Allegretto.
dolce

MARY.
And will com - fort them.
JOHN.
And will com - fort them.
PETER.
turn their mourning in-to joy,
CHORUS.
Weep-ing may en-dure for a
Weep-ing may en -
JESUS.
62 Recit.
Bless-ed are the meek; for
night,
- dure for a night,
But joy com-eth in the morn-ing.
But joy com-eth in the morn-ing.
62 Andante.
colla parte

A
a tempo
they shall in-her-it the earth.
MARY.
mf
p
In the Lord;
JOHN.
mf
p
In the Lord;
PETER.
mf
p
In the Lord;
CHORUS.
a tempo
p
The meek al-so shall in-crease their joy, and the
a tempo
p
The meek al-so shall in-crease their joy, and the
a tempo
p
The meek al - so shall in-crease their joy, and the
a tempo
p
The meek al-so shall in-crease their joy,
a tempo
p

63
Recit.
A
mf
Blessed are they which do
mf
dim.
pp
In the Ho-ly One of Is - ra-el.
mf
dim.
pp
In the Ho-ly One of Is - ra-el.
mf
dim.
pp
In the Ho-ly One of Is - ra-el.
pp
63
poor a-mong men shall re - joice.
pp
poor a-mong men shall re - joice.
pp
poor a-mong men shall re - joice.
pp
dim.
and the poor a - mong men shall re - joice.
63 Andante.
pp
pp colla parte
rit.
dolce
hun - ger and thirst af - ter righteousness; for they shall be

a tempo
fill-ed.
MARY.
a tempo pp
Mer - cy and truth are met to-gether; righteousness and peace have kiss'd each other.
JOHN. pp
Mer - cy and truth are met to-gether; righteousness and peace have kiss'd each other.
PETER. pp
Mer - cy and truth are met to-gether; righteousness and peace have kiss'd each other.
JUDAS. pp
Mer - cy and truth are met to-gether; righteousness and peace have kiss'd each other.
a tempo
64
Quasi Recit.
p
cresc.
Bless - ed are the mer - ci - ful; for
CHORUS.
p
dim.
pp
Sow to yourselves in righteousness;
Sow to yourselves in righteousness;
Sow to yourselves in righteousness;
Sow to yourselves in righteousness;
dim.
colla parte

A - -
a tempo
they___ shall ob - tain mer - cy.___
a tempo
SOLI.
He that hath mer - cy on the
He that hath mer - cy on the
He that hath mer - cy on the
CHORUS.
pp a tempo
Reap__ in mer - - cy.
Reap__ in mer - - cy.
Reap__ in mer - - cy.
Reap__ in mer - - cy.
a tempo
pp
poor, hap - - py is he,
poor, hap - py is he,
poor, hap - py is he,
ad lib.
The poor is ha - ted e - ven of his own neighbour; the
colla parte

65 a tempo
SOLI.
mf cantabile
And sa-tis-fy th' af-
pp
rich hath ma-ny friends.
65 a tempo
CHORUS.
pp
Draw out thy soul to the hun-gry,
Draw out thy soul to the hun-gry,
Draw out thy soul to the hun-gry,
a tempo
65
p
SOLI.
-flic-ted soul;
Then shall thy light rise in ob-scur-i-ty.
molto dim.

66 JESUS. Recit.
L
lento. pp
Bless-ed are the pure in heart; for they shall see
pp colla parte
ppp lento.
God.
MARY.
mf
animato
dolce
rit.
Thou art of pur- - er eyes than to be-hold
animato
rit.
MARY.
a tempo
dim.
e - vil.
JOHN.
p
Bless - ed are the un- - de - fil - ed.
PETER.
p
Who can
a tempo
p
PETER.
say, I have made my heart clean?
JUDAS.
ad lib.
The stars are not pure in His
colla voce

67
Quasi Recit.
JESUS.
L
Blessed are the peace makers; for they shall be called the
sight.
CHORUS.
Alto
How much less man.
Bass
How much less man.
colla parte
A
chil - dren of God.
Bless -
Soprano.
The work of righteousness shall be peace.
Alto.
The work of righteousness shall be peace.
Tenor.
The work of righteousness shall be peace.
Bass.
The work of righteousness shall be peace.

- - ed are they which are per - se - cu - ted for righteousness' sake; for
theirs is the kingdom of heaven. Re - - joice and be ex -
pp lento.
f
68
a tempo, poco animato
con molto espress.
lento.
a tempo ♪ = 88.
pp
mf
- ceed - - ing glad, for great is your reward in
R.
colla
ppp
heaven: For so per - se - cu - ted they the
p
Quasi Recit.
Come prima, ♩ = 69.
parte
pp colla parte

69
stringendo
pro - phets which were be - fore you.
sonore
Cl. Viole & Celli.
stringendo
a tempo, poco animato
f marcato
MARY.
Bless - ed are they which have been sor - row-ful for all Thy
JOHN.
Bless - ed are they which have been sor - row-ful for all Thy
PETER.
Bless - ed are they which have been sor - row - ful for all Thy
JUDAS.
Bless - ed are they which have been sor - row - ful for all Thy
CHORUS.
Soprano.
Bless - ed are they which have been sor-row-ful, for
Alto.
Bless - ed are they which have been sor-row-ful, for
Tenor.
Bless - ed are they which have been sor-row-ful, for
Bass.
Bless - ed are they which have been sor-row-ful, for
a tempo, poco animato (♩= 72.)

pp
rit.
70
Come Iª
poco più lento.
mf
espress.
scour - ges,
for they — shall re-
scour - ges,
mf
scour - ges,
for
scour - ges,
dim. molto
they shall rejoice for Thee, when they have seen all Thy glo - - ry,
they shall rejoice for Thee, when they have seen all Thy glo - - ry,
they shall rejoice for Thee, when they have seen all Thy glo - - ry,
they shall rejoice for Thee, when they have seen all Thy glo - - ry,
p dolce

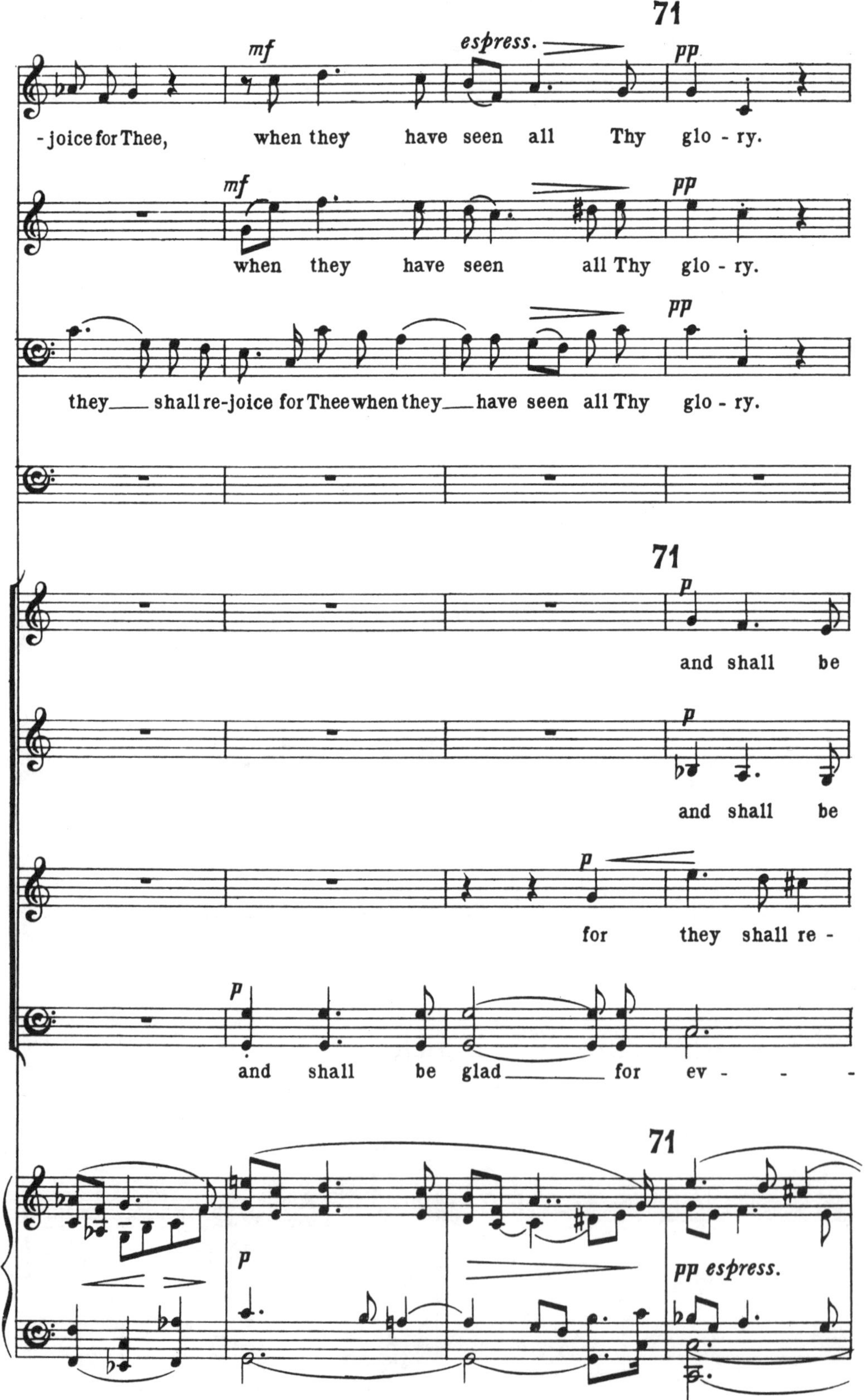
71
mf
espress.
pp
-joice for Thee, when they have seen all Thy glo - ry.
mf
pp
when they have seen all Thy glo - ry.
pp
they shall re-joice for Thee when they have seen all Thy glo - ry.
71
p
and shall be
p
and shall be
p
for they shall re -
p
and shall be glad for ev -
71
p
pp espress.

pp rall.
for ev - - er.
pp rall.
for ev - - er.
pp rall.
for ev - - er.
pp rall.
for ev - - er.
dim. e rit. pp ppp rall.
glad for ev - er, for ev - - er.
dim. e rit. pp ppp rall.
glad, and shall be glad for ev - - er.
dim. e rit. pp ppp rall.
- joice for Thee, they shall re - joice for Thee for ev - - er.
dim. e rit. pp ppp rall.
- er, and shall re - joice for ev - - er.
rall.
dim. e rit. pp ppp

III.

BY THE SEA OF GALILEE.

molto lento.
ev'n - ing was come, He was there a -
dim.
molto lento.
74
mf animato
- lone. And His dis - ci - ples went
pppp
mf animato
rit.
o - - - ver the sea toward Ca - per - - - - - -
rit.
lento.
- - naum.
ppp lento.
attacca.

75
Allegro. ♩=126.
pp
mf espress.
76
simile
dim.
cresc.
p
cresc.
sonore
8
ff
sf
Ped.
dim.
77
MARY MAGDALENE.
con molto espress.
f
dim.
O Lord Al - might - y, God of
R.H.
p
pp
Is - - ra - el, the soul in an - guish, the troubled spi - rit,
p
cresc.
simile
ppp
cresc.

cresc.
f
criー eth unー to Thee. Hear and have mer -
cresc.
p
78
dim.
- cy.
pp
p
79
Hear and have mer - cy, for Thou art mer - - ci - ful:
espress.
p
stringendo
have pit - y up - on me, be - cause I have
stringendo

80
stringendo
sinned be - fore Thee. Hear the
pp
stringendo
dim.
rit
voice of the for-lorn, and de - liv - er me out of my
pp
rit.
81 Tempo I°
fear.
p
Help me, de - so-late
Tempo I°
simile
p
cresc.
pp
f
wo - - man, which have no help - - er but
cresc.
sf

82
Thee, no help - - er but Thee.
p
cresc.
sf
con Ped.
f largamente
largamente
f
poco a poco rit.
Hear and have pit - y, the troubl - ed spi - rit, the
p
poco a poco rit.
ad lib.
Andantino.
soul in anguish cri-eth un-to Thee.
= 120.
Andantino.
ppp
colla parte
pp
83
pp Recit. più mosso.
a tempo
Woe is me! for I am as when they have gathered the
ppp colla parte
Andantino.
Recit.
più mosso.
p
sum - mer fruits, as the
pp
pp colla parte

grape-gleanings of the vint-age. *ten.* Have

♪ = 100. *ppp* *dolciss.*

84 *Allegro molto.* *agitato* *rit.* *Lento.*

pit-y, be-cause I have sinned be-fore Thee. My

Allegro molto. ♩ = 126. *cresc.* *rit.* *Lento.*

Allegro. *p* *lento.* **85** *Lento.*

tears run down like a riv- - - er day and night.

Allegro. *cresc.* *pp* *sf* *Lento.*

pp *dolce*

What-so-ev- - er mine

pp *pp colla parte*

animato

eyes de-sired I kept not from them,

pp

Ped. *

86 Allegro. cresc. poco accel. f
I with-held not my heart from a-ny joy.
Soprano.
Alto.
pp sotto voce
Let us
CHORUS.
Tenor.
Bass.
pp sotto voce
Let us
86 Allegro. ♩. = 100.
ppp
poco accel.
87
♩. = 112.
fill our-selves with cost-ly wine, let us
pp sotto voce
Let us fill our-selves with cost-ly wine,
ppp
fill our-selves with cost-ly wine, let us
87
♩. = 112.

agitato
p
"Ye that
fill ourselves with costly wine and ointments,
fill ourselves with costly wine and ointments,
f
kindle a fire, walk in the flame
cresc.
cre - scen - do -

88
of your fire,
pp
Let us fill our-selves with
pp
Let us fill our-selves with
88
ppp
p
walk a-mong the brands that ye have
cost-ly wine and oint - ments,
p
Let no flow'r of the spring pass
cost-ly wine and oint - ments,
p
Let
8

f
kindled. This shall ye have of Mine

p
Let us crown ___ our-selves ___ with

p
by us, Let us crown ___ our-selves with

no flow'r of the spring pass by us, Let us crown,

89

ff molto agitato
hand." God of Is - - ra-el, ___

p
rose - - - buds, let us

cresc. ff
rose - - - buds, let us crown ___ our-selves, ___

cresc. ff
let us crown ___ our-selves, ___

crown our-selves with rose - buds, ___

89

pp giocoso

ff
the soul in an - guish the troubled
p
crown our-selves,
let us crown our - selves with rose - buds
p
crown
p
with
p
crown
p
f
crown
our-selves
pp
f
90
spi-rit cri-eth un - to Thee.
Hear
ff
before they be with - - ered.
ff
rose - buds before they be with - - ered.
cresc.
ff
ourselves,
ff
before they be with - - ered.
90
ff
ffz
ff

dim.
and have mer - cy.
ppp
Let us fill our - selves with
Let us fill our - selves with
Let us fill our - selves with
Let us fill our - selves with
ppp
espress. p
Hear and have mer - cy.
cost - ly wine and oint - - - - ments, with
cost - ly wine and oint - - - - ments, with
cost - ly wine and oint - - - - ments, with
cost - ly wine and oint - - - -

p poco a poco rit.
Hear and have mer - - cy.
oint - - - ments, and let no flow'r of the spring pass by
oint - - - ments, and let no flow'r of the spring pass by
oint - - - ments, and let no flow'r of the spring pass by
- - - - - ments, let no flow'r of the spring,
poco a poco rit.
91 Andantino.
p
The
us.
us, no flow-er pass by us.
us.
in 6
no flow-er pass by us.
Andantino. ♪ = 120.
91
p

Recit.

mirth___ of tab-rets ceas-eth;___ the noise of

colla parte

92 *a tempo*

them that re - joice___ end - eth,___

dim.

Our__ dance is turn - ed in - to mourn - ing.___

accel.

pp

pp accel.

93 Moderato.

Moderato. ♩= 80.

93

ppp

Recit. rit.

p

"This shall ye have of Mine hand,

pp

colla parte

Recit.

pp molto espress.

ten.

ye shall lie down in

Lento.

a tempo

rit.

pp

Più lento.

sor - - - row." Hear and have

a tempo, Lento.

pp espress.

rit.

Più lento.

ppp

dim.

mer - cy, for Thou art mer - - ci -

dim.

94
(There arose a great tempest in the sea.)
- ful.
Più mosso.
sf
stringendo - - -
p R.H.
Ped.
- - - - - al - - - Allegro. ♩. = 132.
sf
p cresc. mf
Ped.
95
cresc.
fz
sf
p cresc.
sfp
Ped.
Ped.
cresc.

96
fp
ffz
MARY MAGDALENE.
mf
Is Thy wrath against the sea?
p
cresc.
The voice of Thy thund - er is in the
sfp
cresc.
heav - ens!
fffz
ffz

97
f
Deep call-eth un-to deep at the
p
ten.
Ped. Ped. Ped. Ped. Ped. Ped.
noise of Thy cat - aracts.
sf
ten.
Ped. Ped. Ped. Ped. Ped. Ped.
I see a ship in the midst of the sea, dis -
pp
sfp
-tress'd with waves: And One com - eth
dim.
Vl.II.

98

un - to it,

pp

walk - - ing on the sea! And

cresc.

ppp

they that are in the ship, toil - ing in row - - ing,

Horns

Ped. ✱Ped. ✱Ped. ✱Ped. ✱Ped. ✱Ped. ✱

99

Quick

are trou - bled and cry out for

Ped. ✱Ped. ✱Ped. ✱Ped. ✱Ped. ✱Ped. ✱

fear.
Tenor. THE APOSTLES. (In the ship.)
CHORUS.
It, — it is a
Bass.
It, it is a
Strings.
JESUS.
poco rit.
100
Poco meno mosso.
Be of
spi - - - rit!
spi - - - - rit!
100 Poco meno mosso.
poco rit.
pp ♩. = 116.
good cheer, it is I,

accel.

be not a - - fraid.

accel.

101 PETER. *f* *impetuoso* *allargando* *a tempo*

Lord, if it be Thou, bid me

8

f a tempo *ff* 3 *colla parte*

3

come un-to Thee up-on the wa - - ters.

f espress. *p*

JESUS. 102 Recit. *ad lib.* *a tempo*

Come!

a tempo

f *pp* *ff*

JUDAS.
Fear-
-fulness and trembling are come up-on him, and an hor-ri-ble dread
CHORUS.
Tenor.
THE APOSTLES.
He walk-eth on the waters,
Fear-fulness and trembling are come up-on him, and an hor-ri-ble dread hath o-ver-
Bass.
He walk-eth on the waters,
Fear-fulness and trembling are come up-on him, and an hor-ri-ble dread hath o-ver-
cre-scen-do

103
largamente
PETER.
Lord,
hath o - ver - whelmed him.
- whelmed him.
- whelmed him.
103
L
MARY MAGDALENE.
PETER.
He
save me, I per-ish!
poco tranquillo
Più lento.
rit.
stretch - eth forth His hand.
Più lento. ♩. = 112
rit.

104
JESUS.
pp
O thou of lit - tle faith, wherefore didst thou doubt?
Andante.
♩ = 56.
pp
MARY MAGDALENE.
p
The wind ceas-eth and they wor - ship Him.
Tenor.
p
Of a truth Thou art the
Bass.
THE APOSTLES.
Of a truth Thou art the
CHORUS.
pp
dim.
MARY MAGDALENE.
p solenne
They wor - ship Him.
105
PETER, JOHN & JUDAS.
p
The Lord hath His
Tenor.
pp
Son of God,
Thou art the
Bass I.
Son of God,
Thou art the
Bass II.
Son of God,
Thou art the
ppp

way in the whirl - - wind and in the storm. Thou art the
Son of God, of a truth Thou art the Son of God, Thou art the
Son of God, of a truth Thou art the Son of God,
Son of God, Thou art the Son of God,
pp
pp
106
MARY MAGDALENE.
dim.
pp
Son of God.
They wor - - ship Him.
T.
dim.
Son of God.
B.
p
Thou art the Son of God.
106
espress.
morendo
pp

107
MARY MAGDALENE.
Recit.
a tempo
Recit.
cresc.
Who stilleth the raging of the seas,
Who maketh the storm a
Moderato.
colla parte
a tempo
colla parte
Poco più mosso.
a tempo
calm?
Thy pro - vi - dence, O
Poco più mosso. ♩ = 84.
a tempo
Fa-ther, governeth it:
animato
for Thou hast made a way in the sea,
A
animato
108
marcato
and a safe path in the waves;
Ped.

p
Shew - ing that Thou canst save from all dan - ger.
dim.
p
dim.
Ped.
stringendo
p
109 a tempo
Thy face, Lord, will I seek.
stringendo
pp
a tempo
Ped. Ped.
Ped. Ped.
Thou hast not for - sak - - en them that seek Thee.
Ped. Ped.
dolce
stringendo
Thy face, Lord, will I seek.
p
stringendo
cresc.
p
Ped.

f
My soul fol-low-eth hard,
cresc.
p
f
110
molto rit.
ff a tempo
hard af - ter Thee: Thy right - hand up-hold-eth
molto rit.
ff a tempo
dim.
con Ped.
accel. molto
p rit. molto espress. pp
me. Thy face, Lord, will I seek, Thy face, Lord, will I
accel. molto
seek.
Lento. ♩= 80.
a tempo
pp
rit.

IN CÆSAREA PHILIPPI.

111 *Andantino.*

Tenor Recit. *p*

When Je - sus came in - to the parts of Cæ - sa - re - a Phil - ip - pi, — He ask - - ed His dis - ci - ples, say - ing:

Andantino. ♩ = 72.

p *rit.*

pp colla parte

JESUS. Recit. *accel.*

Whom do men say that I, the Son of man, am?

♩ = 80.

colla parte *accel.*

112 Allegro moderato.
Tenor I.
cresc.
Some say John the Bap-tist: some, E-li- - -as; and
Tenor II.
Some say John the Bap-tist: some, E-li- - -as; and
Bass I.
Some say John the Bap-tist: some, E-li- - -as; and
Bass II.
and
CHORUS.
Allegro moderato. ♩=116.
pp
dim.
rit. al -
others, Je-re-mi-as, or one of the prophets.
espress.
113 Andante. Quasi Recit.
JESUS.
But whom say ye that I am?
PETER.
Thou art the
Andante. ♩=80.
largamente
cresc.

a tempo
lento
Bless - - ed art thou,
Christ, the Son of the liv - ing God.
Moderato.
espress. dolciss. Recit.
Si-mon Bar-Jo-na: for flesh and blood hath not re-veal-ed it un-to thee,
colla parte
114 a tempo
molto espress.
but My Father Which is in heaven. Thou art
♩= 60.
a tempo
cresc.
con Ped.
dim.
115 Moderato. ♩= 72.
Pe-ter, and up - - on this rock I will build My
Moderato.
colla parte

cresc.
Church; and the gates of hell shall not prevail a-
cresc.
rit.
116
-gainst it.
Lento e solenne.
Soprano.
Alto.
Tenor.
Bass.
SOLI & CHORUS.
Proclaim un-to them that dwell on the
Proclaim un-to them that dwell on the
Pro- - claim un-to them, pro-claim
Proclaim un-to them that dwell, pro-
Lento e solenne. ♩=52.
Ped.
Ped.
cresc.
poco
earth, and un-to ev'- - ry na- - tion,
earth, and un-to ev'- - ry na- - tion, to
un-to them, to them that dwell on the earth, and un-to
them that dwell
-claim un-to them that dwell on the earth, and un-to ev'-ry
Ped.
Ped.
Ped.
Ped.

- a - poco - - - - - R- - - - - -

and kindred, and tongue, the ev-er-

ev'-ry nation, and tongue, and kin-dred, and tongue, the ev-er-

ev'-ry na-tion, and kin-dred, and tongue, the ev-er-last-ing

na-tion, and kin-dred, and tongue, the ev-er-

f

R

ffz

Ped. * Ped. * Ped. * Ped. * Ped. * Ped. *

117

- al - - -

fff

lunga

-last-ing Gos-pel.

fff

-last-ing Gos-pel.

fff

ev-er-last-ing Gos-pel.

fff

lunga

-last-ing Gos-pel.

117

lunga

fff

JESUS.
Quasi Recit. ♩= 60.
p
And I will give un-to thee the keys of the king-dom of
pp colla parte
118
cresc.
ff marcato
heaven: And what-so - ev-er thou shalt bind on earth, shall be bound in
mf solenne
L
pp
dolciss. ♩= 50.
heaven: And what-so - ev - er thou shalt loose on earth, shall be
pp
ppp
L
119
loosed in hea-ven.
ppp

MARY MAGDALENE.
poco animato
pp
Thy face, Lord, will I seek; My soul followeth
♩ = 72.
poco animato
ppp
cresc.
pp R
hard af - ter Thee; Help me, de - so-late wo - man.
f
pp colla parte
Andante. ♩ = 69.
120
MARY.
pp espress. ad lib.
dolce e cantabile
Heark - en, O daughter: When thou art in
Andante.
Clar. espress.
pp
ppp
cresc.
trib - u-la-tion, If thou turn to the Lord thy God, And

shall be o - be-di - ent un-to His voice, He will not for-
dim. rit.
121 ad lib.
pp
- sake thee. Heark - en, O daugh - ter; Come
colla parte
pp
a tempo
R
pp
thou, for there is peace to thee, peace to
a tempo
pp
122 Tranquillo.
thee.
TENOR. quasi Recit. p espress.
She stood at His feet
122 Tranquillo. ♩ = 68.
pp
ppp

weep - ing, and be-gan to wash His feet with tears, and did
wipe them with the hairs of her head,
123 Più mosso.
p marcato
This Man,
S.
CHORUS, WOMEN.
C.
p marcato
This Man,
123 Più mosso. ♩.=84.
ppp
pp
animato
sf p
if He were a pro - phet, would have known who and what
sf p
if He were a pro - phet, would have known who
animato
tr
cresc.
f

124
man - ner of wo - man this is
cresc.
and what man - ner of wo - man this is
p
124
p
p
ff
that toucheth Him: for she is a sin-
ff
that toucheth Him: for she is a sin-
p
fp
sf
sf
f
- ner.
- ner.
R
p
dim.
pp

125 Tranquillo.
Tenor.
p
And kissed His feet, and a-noint-ed them with the
Tranquillo. ♩= 63.
MARY MAGDALENE.
pp espress.
Hide not Thy face far from me;
ointment.
Clar.
Fl.
L.H.
pppp
put not Thy servant a-way in an-ger.
L
Oboe.
p molto espress.
dim.

126 JESUS. *p*

Thy sins are for - giv - - - en; Thy faith hath sav - - - ed thee; Go in peace.

molto espress. *rit.* *a tempo* *dolce* Clar. *rit. molto* *lunga.* *pp* *fp*

STAND

127 *pp*

128 Allegretto tranquillo.
Soprano.
pp dolce e legato
Turn you to the stronghold, ye pris - on-ers of hope. To the
Alto.
pp dolce e legato
Turn you to the stronghold, ye pris - on-ers of hope. To the
Tenor.
pp dolce e legato
Turn you to the stronghold, ye pris - on-ers of hope. To the
Bass.
pp dolce e legato
Turn you to the stronghold, ye pris - on-ers of hope. To the
CHORUS.
128 Allegretto tranquillo. ♩ = 88.
pp
pp dolce e legato
Lord our God belong mercies and for - give - ness-es,
Lord our God belong mercies and for - give - ness-es,
Lord our God belong mercies and for - give - ness-es,
Lord our God belong mercies and for - give - ness-es,

* To be sung by the Soloist taking the part of "Peter."

130
hope.
hope.
hope.
hope.
mf cantabile
Mak -
mf cantabile
The fear of the Lord is a crown of wis - dom,
130
mf dolce ed espress.
mf cantabile
Both which are the
dim.
mf
- ing peace and per - fect health to flourish; Both which
mf
a crown of wis - dom,

mf cantabile
The fear of the Lord is a
gifts of God: The fear of the
are the gifts of God:
mf
legatissimo
the fear of the Lord, the fear of the
131
mf
legatissimo
crown of wis - dom, and it en - largeth their re -
f
Lord is a crown of wis - dom, it en - larg - eth their re -
p
mf
is a crown, and it en - larg - eth their re -
Lord is a crown of wis - dom, and it en - larg - eth their re -
131
largamente
f

SOLI.

dolce

p Turn you to the stronghold.

p Turn you to the stronghold, ye pris - on-ers of hope. *dim.*

p Turn you to the stronghold, ye pris - on-ers of hope. *dim.*

p Turn you to the stronghold, ye pris - on-ers of hope. *dim.*

CHORUS.

dim -joicing that love Him. *p* Turn you,

dim. -joic - ing that love Him. *p*

dim. -joic - ing that love Him. *p* Turn you,

dim. *p* -joicing that love Him. *p* Turn you,

dim. *p* *dim.*

132

pp ye pris - oners of hope. *poco rit.* *dim.*

espress. *pp* Turn you, turn you, turn you, ye prisoners of hope.

pp Turn, ye pris - oners of hope, ye

pp Turn, ye

132

ppp *poco rit.*

133
a tempo
espress.
To the Lord our God belong
To the Lord our God belong mer-
To the Lord our God belong mer-
To the Lord our God belong
SOLI.
133
a tempo
Turn you.
Turn you.
pris - oners of hope.
pris - oners of hope.
CHORUS.
133
a tempo

p
mer-cies and for - give - ness-es,
p
- - cies and for - give - ness-es,
p
Though
p
- - cies and for - give - ness-es,
p
Though
p
mer-cies and for - give - ness-es,
p
Though
mf espress. dim. p
Though we have re - belled a - gainst
p mf espress. dim. p
Though we have re - belled a-gainst Him,
pp p mf espress. dim. p
Turn you. Though we have re - belled a-gainst Him,
pp p mf espress. dim. p
Turn you. Though we have re - belled a-gainst Him,
mf

mf
p
dim.
Though we have re - belled a - gainst Him,
we have re - belled against Him,
pp
though
we have re - belled a - gainst Him,
though
we have re - belled a - gainst Him,
though
Him,
though we have re - belled a - gainst
though we have re - belled a-gainst Him;
though we have re - belled a-gainst Him;
though we have re - belled a - gainst Him;

134
poco rit.
pp
a tempo
though we have re - belled a - gainst Him;
we have re - belled a - gainst Him;
we have re-belled a - gainst Him;
we have re - belled a - gainst Him;
poco rit.
pp
134 a tempo
Him;
mf cantabile
Thou art a God of the af -
134
pp poco rit.
mf a tempo
CHORUS.
mf cantabile
Thou
mf cantabile
Thou art an help - er of the op - press - ed,
- flict - ed,
mf
Thou art a

art an up - - hold - er of the weak,
legato
Thou art an up-hold - er of the weak, Thou art the God
God, Thou art a God of the af - flicted, Thou art a protect - or
mf cantabile
Thou art a pro-tect - or, a pro -
135 molto largamente
f cantabile
A Sa - viour of them that are with -
cresc.
of the af - flict - - ed, A Sa - viour of them that are
cresc.
mf
of the for - lorn, A Sa - viour of them that are with -
cresc.
mf
- tect - or of the for - lorn, A Sa - viour of them that are with -
135
cresc.
f
molto largamente

SOLI.
Turn you to the stronghold, ye pris - oners of hope.
Turn you to the stronghold, ye pris - oners of hope.
Turn you to the stronghold, ye pris - oners of hope.
Turn you to the stronghold, ye pris - oners of hope.
CHORUS.
- out hope.
with - out hope.
- out hope.
- out hope.
p cresc. molto

136
ff
dim.
p
espress.
3
dim.
Bless - ed is he who is not fall - en from his hope in the Lord.
pp
For

pp
For He will for-give their in-i-qui-ty.
pp
For He will for-give their in-i-qui-ty.
pp
For He will for-give their in-i-qui-ty.
pp
For He will for-give their in-i-qui-ty.
poco
He will for-give their in-i-quity, and He will re-mem-ber their
poco
He will for-give their in-i-quity, and He will re-mem-ber their
poco
He will for-give their in-i-quity, and He will re-mem-ber their
poco
He will for-give their in-i-quity, and He will re-mem-ber their

137
pp
Turn you to the stronghold.
pp
Turn you to the strong - hold.
pp
Turn you to the strong - - hold.
pp
Turn you to the strong - hold.
137
ppp
sin no more, He will re - mem - ber their sin no
ppp
sin no more, He will re - mem - ber their sin no
ppp
sin no more, He will re - mem - ber their sin no
ppp
sin no more, He will re - mem - ber their sin no
137
ppp

138
p espress.
Turn you,
p
Turn, ye prisoners of
pp
dim.
Turn you to the stronghold.
p
Turn you to the
pp
dim.
Turn you to the stronghold.
p
Turn you to the
138
more.
more.
mf espress. dim.
p
more.
Turn, ye prisoners.
mf espress.
dim.
p
more.
Turn you, turn, ye prisoners.
138
pp
dim.
mf
dim.
p

139
dim.
rit.
pp a tempo
f
turn, ye pris- - oners of hope.
rit.
p
pp
f
hope, turn, ye prisoners of hope.
dim.
rit.
pp
f
strong - hold, ye pris- - oners of hope.
dim.
rit.
pp
f
strong - hold, ye pris- - oners of hope.
139
pp
rit.
a tempo
f
Turn, ye pris- - oners of hope.
pp
f
Turn, ye pris- - oners of hope.
pp
f
Turn, ye pris- - oners of hope.
pp
f
Turn, ye pris- - oners of hope.
139
rit.
a tempo
dim.
pp
cresc. molto
ff

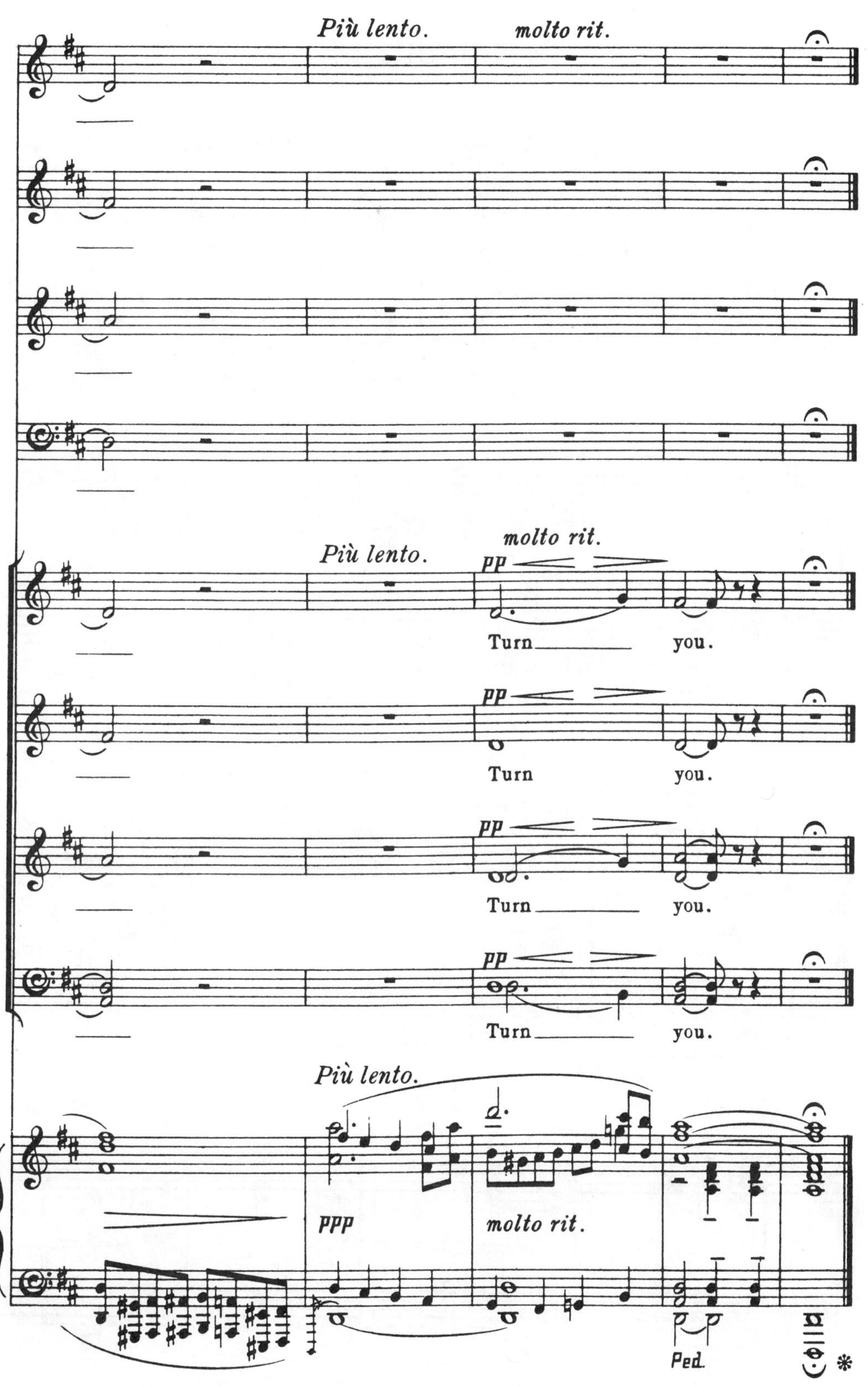

End of Part I.

PART II.

INTRODUCTION.

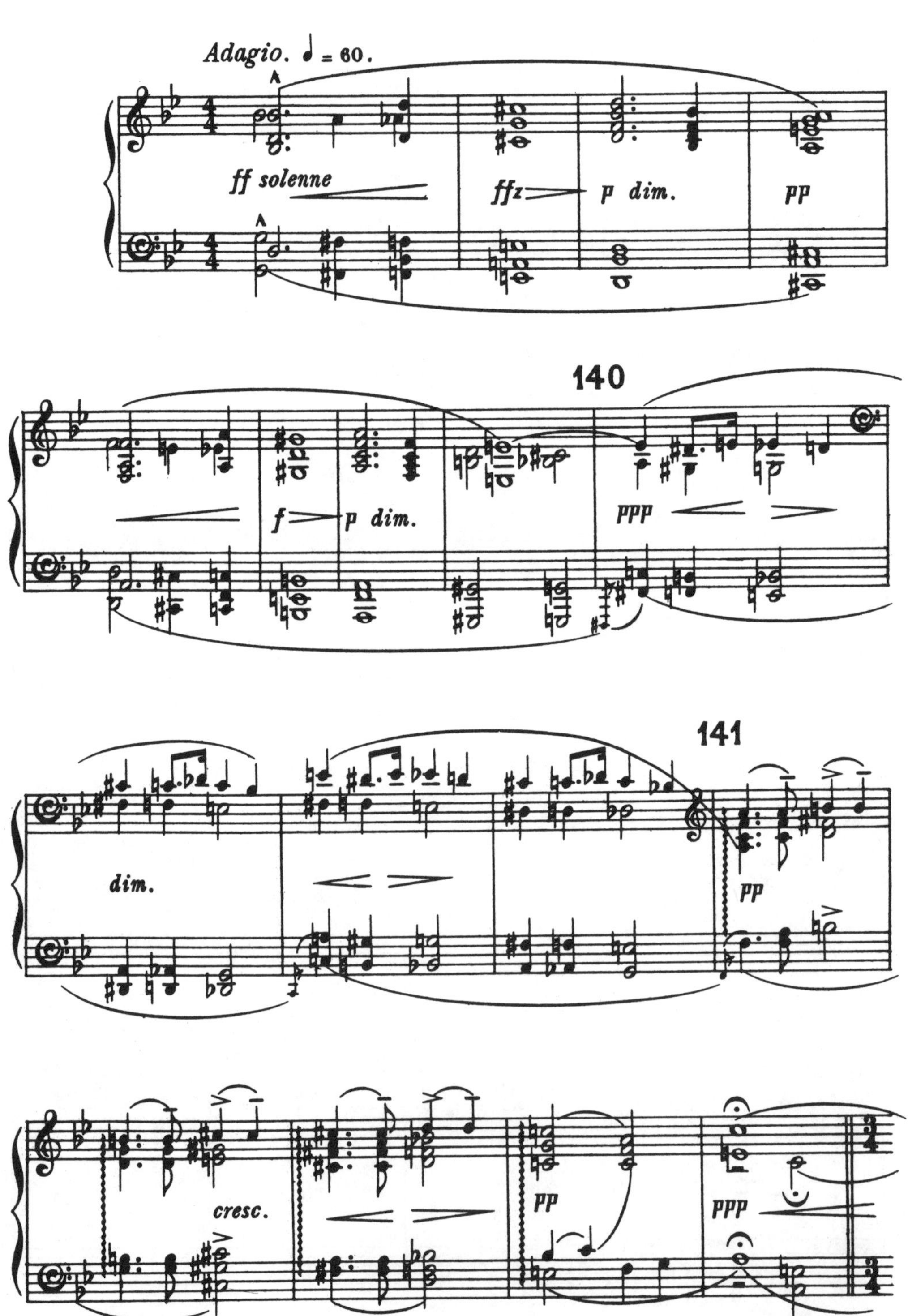

142 Poco più mosso. ♩= 66.
f
allargando
143 Più lento. ♩= 60.
rit.
pp
dim.
ppp
144 Adagio.
molto rit.
mesto
ppp

IV.

THE BETRAYAL.

146 *Più lento.*

SOLO TENOR.

p And He be-gan to teach them, that the Son of man *molto espress.* must suf-fer ma-ny things, *cresc.* and be re-jected, *R* *pp* and be killed.

CHORUS.

Soprano. *pp mistico* "I will smite the Shep-herd, and the sheep of the flock *pp* shall be scatter'd."

Alto. *pp* "I will smite the Shep-herd, and the sheep of the flock *pp* shall be scatter'd."

Tenor. *pp* "I will smite the Shep-herd, and the sheep of the flock *pp* shall be scatter'd a-broad." *ppp*

Bass. *pp* "I will smite the Shep-herd, and the sheep of the flock *pp* shall be scatter'd a-broad." *ppp*

146 *Più lento.*

p *ppp*

147 Andante.
PETER.
Be it far from Thee, Lord, this shall never be unto Thee Though all men shall be offended because of Thee, yet will I never be offended.
CHORUS.
THE APOSTLES.
JOHN & Tenors.
Though we should die with Thee, yet will we not deny Thee, yet will we not deny Thee.
JUDAS & Basses.
Though we should die with Thee, yet will we not deny Thee, Though we should die with Thee, yet will we not deny Thee.
147 Andante. ♩ = 76.
cresc.
cresc. e stringendo
lunga

148 *Allegro moderato.*

Tenor. Quasi Recit.*

Then gathered the chief Priests and Phar-i-sees a coun-cil, and said:

Bass.*

Then gathered the chief Priests and Phar-i-sees a coun-cil, and said:

148 *Allegro moderato.* ♩ = 108.

sf*p

p cresc. molto sf

Tenor I.

"What do we? what do we? For this Man do-eth many

Tenor II.

"What do we? what do we? For this Man do-eth many

Bass I.

"What do we? what do we? For this Man do-eth many

Bass II.

"What do we? what do we? This Man do-eth many

* The Chord should be sustained for sometime before the voices enter.

mi - - ra-cles."
mi - ra-cles."
mi - - ra-cles."
mi - - ra-cles."
p cresc. molto
sf
149
Tenor. Quasi Recit.*
dim.
R
So from that day forth they took counsel that they might put Him to
* Bass.
So from that day forth they took counsel that they might put Him to
colla parte
espress.
dim.
pp
150
Più lento.
pp
death. Then entered Satan in-to Judas,
death. Then entered Satan in-to Judas,
150 Più lento. ♩=96.
L
Cl. & Fag.
pp
mf

* The Chord should be sustained for sometime before the voices enter.

a tempo
p
And he went his way, and com-mun-ed with the
p
And he went his way, and com-mun-ed with the
a tempo, ♩ = 108.
sfp
pp
cresc.
f
151
chief Priests and Cap - - tains.
cresc.
f
chief Priests and Cap - - tains.
151
cresc.
ff
fz
ffz
JUDAS.
p parlando
What are ye willing to
Brass.
pp
L
p
pp
ppp colla parte

pp
give me, and I will de - liv-er Him — un - to you?
Harp.
Clar.
152
CHORUS.
Tenor. p a tempo
And — they weigh-ed un - to him thir - ty
Bass. p a tempo
And — they weigh-ed un - to him thir - ty
152
ppp a tempo
pie - ces of sil - ver.
pie - ces of sil - ver.
cresc.

153
f
Judas
Judas
ffz
sf p
then, having re-ceiv - - ed a band of men and of-fi-cers,
cresc.
marziale
p
com - eth,
com - eth
pp
with lanterns and
com - eth
with lanterns and

JUDAS.
154
f rhapsodically.
(Let Him make speed, and hasten His work, that we may
torches and weapons.
torches and weapons.
154
p
see it;
con entusiasmo
He shall
mf
fp
bear the glo - ry, and shall sit and
rule up-on His throne, up-on His
155
impetuoso
ff
marcato

ff
throne, the great King, the
f
ff
p
ff
dim. 156
Lord of the whole earth.)
CHORUS.
Tenor.
pp
with torches and weapons.
Bass.
pp
with torches and weapons.
156
dim.
ppp
JUDAS. parlando
p
Whom - - - so - ev - - er I shall kiss, that
ppp
same is He: hold Him fast.

157 L'istesso tempo.
cresc.
sf
JUDAS.
f
Hail,
R
JESUS.
158 Lento. Recit.
Whom seek ye?
Mas - ter!
CHORUS.
Tenor.
Allegro.
Je - sus of Nazar-eth.
Bass.
Je - sus of Nazar-eth.
158 Lento.
Allegro.
rit.
mf
pp
Andante.
JESUS.
mf
dolce
I am He; if there-fore ye seek Me, let these go
Andante. ♩ = 63.
p

159
their way.
SOLO CONTRALTO. Recit.
And they all for-sook Him and
Lento.
159
ppp
fled; But Pe-ter fol-low'd Him a-far off to see the end.
pp
pp
pp
ppp
Allegro.
Tenor.
CHORUS.
R
And they that had laid hands on
Bass.
And they that had laid hands on
Allegro. ♩= 108.
R
pp
sfp
a tempo; feroce
Je-sus, led Him a-way to the
ff
Je-sus, led Him a-way to the
a tempo; feroce
f

High Priest.
High Priest.
rf
160
pp
CHORUS.
Tenor.
Bass.
pp
With lanterns, and
dim.
dim.
torch-es, and wea-pons.
Alto.
mf
THE SERVANTS. Thou
poco rit.
dolce
poco rit.
p

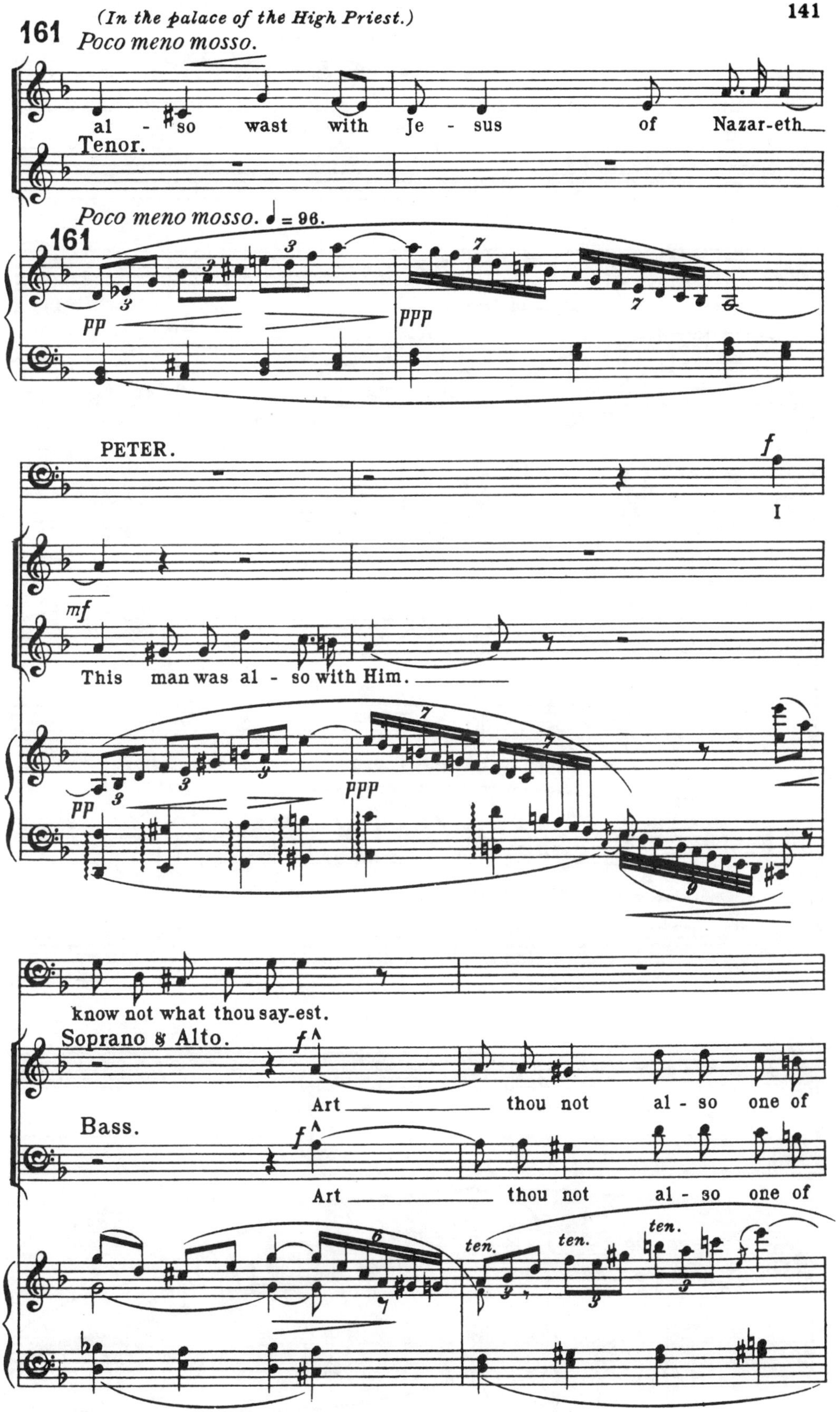

161
(In the palace of the High Priest.)
Poco meno mosso.
al - so wast with Je - sus of Nazar-eth
Tenor.
Poco meno mosso. ♩= 96.
161
pp
ppp
PETER.
f
I
mf
This man was al - so with Him.
pp
ppp
know not what thou say-est.
Soprano & Alto.
f
Art thou not al - so one of
Bass.
f
Art thou not al - so one of
ten.
ten.
ten.

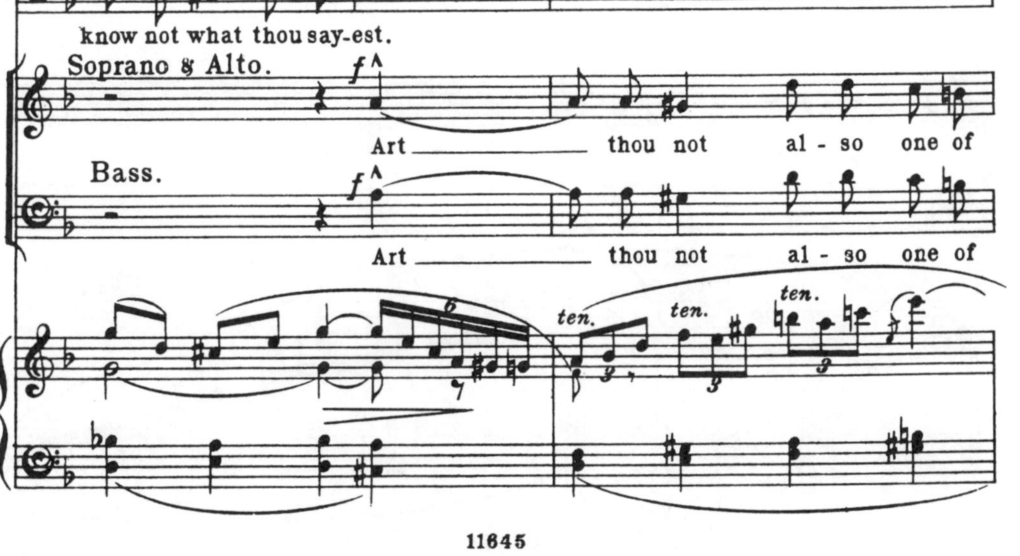

R
162
As thy soul liveth, I am not.
His dis - ciples?
His dis - ciples?
Did
R
162
Soprano & Tenor.
Sure -
a tempo
we not see thee in the gar - den with Him?
a tempo
ten.
ten.
ten.
- ly thou al - so art one of them.
ten.
ten.
ten.

PETER.
Quasi Recit.
R
I swear by the Lord; I know not this Man of whom ye
colla parte
fp colla parte
sf
sf sf
163 (♩ = 88)
speak.
L
♩ = 96.
a tempo
espress. e sostenuto
p
ff
p
Soprano.
Quasi Recit.
CHORUS.
Then led they
Alto.
Then led they
a tempo
rit.
pp
R
Je - sus un-to the hall of judg-ment.
Je - sus un-to the hall of judg-ment.
a tempo
rit.
a tempo
dim.
pp

164 Adagio.
Soprano I.
Soprano II.
Contralto I.
Contralto II.
CHORUS.
And the Lord turn-ed and look'd up-on Pe-ter, And
And the Lord turn-ed and look'd up-on Pe-ter, And
And the Lord turn - ed and look'd up - on Pe-ter, And
And the Lord turn - ed and look'd up - on Pe-ter, And
164 Adagio. ♩=66.
cresc.
165
molto espress.
he went out, and wept, he went out, and wept,
he went out, and wept, and wept, went out, and
he went out, and wept, he went out, he went out, and wept,
he went out, and wept, wept, wept,
165

stringendo molto
cresc.
rit.
molto dim.
wept bit - ter-ly,
166
wept bit-ter-ly, wept bit-ter - ly.
Lento.
espress.
colla parte
CONTRALTO.
Recit.
ad lib.
Then Ju-das, which had betrayed Him, when he saw that He was condemn'd, re-

167
Moderato.
a tempo
-pen-ted him-self, and brought a - gain the thir-ty pie-ces of sil-ver
THE SINGERS, (within the Temple)
pp
O Lord God, to Whom ven - geance be-long - - eth,
O Lord God, to Whom ven - geance be-long - - eth,
O Lord God, to Whom ven - geance be-long - - eth,
CHORUS.
167 Moderato. 𝅗𝅥 = 54.
a tempo
pp
to the chief Priests and El- ders.
Lift up Thyself, Thou Judge of the earth. O Lord God, to Whom
Lift up Thyself, Thou Judge of the earth. O Lord God, to Whom
Lift up Thyself, Thou Judge of the earth. O Lord God, to Whom
O Lord God, to Whom
cresc.
p
marcato

dim.
vengeance belong-eth, Ren-der a re - ward to the proud.
vengeance belong-eth, Ren-der a re - ward to the proud.
vengeance belong-eth, Ren - der a re - ward to the proud.
vengeance belong-eth, Ren - der a re - ward to the proud.
8va bassa
168
JUDAS.
My pun-ish-ment
Lord, how long shall the wick - ed, how long, how long shall the
Lord, how long shall the wick - ed, how long, how long shall the
Lord, how long shall the wick - ed, how long, how long shall the
Lord, how long shall the wick - ed, how long, how long shall the
168

espress.
is greater than I can bear.
wick - ed triumph?
cresc.
wick - ed triumph? How long shall they ut - ter and speak hard
cresc.
wick - ed triumph? How long shall they ut - ter and speak hard
cresc.
wick - ed triumph? How long shall they ut - ter and speak hard
p cresc.
pesante
Mine in - i - qui - ty is greater than can be for-
Soprano I e II. pp
They
p
dim.
pp
things? And all the workers of in - i - qui - ty boast them - selves? They
p
dim.
things? And all the workers of in - i - qui - ty boast them - selves?
p
dim.
things? And all the workers of in - i - qui - ty boast them - selves?
p
dim.
8va bassa

169
dim.
-giv - en.
Soprano I.
break in pie - ces Thy people, O Lord, And af - flict Thine
Soprano II.
break in pie - ces Thy people, O Lord, And af - flict Thine
Alto I.
break in pie - ces Thy people, O Lord, And af - flict Thine
Alto II.
break in pie - ces Thy people, O Lord, And af - flict Thine
Tenor.
THE PRIESTS.
mf parlando
A voice of trembling, of fear, - Why art thou so grieved in thy
Bass.
mf parlando
A voice of trembling, of fear, - Why art thou so grieved in thy
169
L'istesso tempo. Quasi Recit.
cresc.
dim.
I have sinned in that I have betray-ed the in-no-cent blood.
molto dim.
her - i - tage.
her - i - tage.
her - i - tage.
her - i - tage.
mind?
mind?
L'istesso tempo. ♩=108.
colla parte

170
Tenor.
a tempo
cresc.
ff
What is that, what is that to us? See
Bass.
f
cresc.
ff
What is that, what to us? See
170
a tempo
f
cresc.
JUDAS.
Recit.
R
ff
dim.
p
I have sin-ned,— I have be-
fz
thou to that.
fz
thou to that.
colla parte
fz pp
CONTRALTO.
171
A
a tempo
f
ff
And he cast down the
pp
3
-tray-ed the in-no-cent
fff
Se - -lah!
fff
Se - -lah!
171
A
a tempo
8
3
ffz
mf

ff
pie - ces of sil - ver and de-part - - - -
Soprano.
Alto.
ff
Se - - - - lah!
ff
Se - - - - lah!
8
sf mf
sf cresc.
172
- - - - ed.
ff
Lord, how long shall the
ff
Lord, how long shall the
THE SINGERS.
ff
Lord, how long shall the
ff
Lord, how long shall the
172
𝅗𝅥 = 54.
ff pesante

ff dim.
wick - ed tri - umph? Yet they say, The Lord shall not see;
wick - ed tri - umph? Yet they say, The Lord shall not see;
wick - ed tri - umph? Yet they say, The Lord shall not see;
wick - ed tri - umph? Yet they say, The Lord shall not see;
mf
dim.
He that plant - ed the ear, shall He not hear?
He that plant - ed the ear, shall He not hear?
He that plant - ed the ear, shall He not hear?
He that plant - ed the ear, shall He not hear?
p
p dim.
pp
He that form - ed the eye, shall He not see?
He that form - ed the eye, shall He not see?
He that form - ed the eye, shall He not see?
He that form - ed the eye, shall He not see?
R

173 Più lento.
JUDAS.
p
Whither shall I go from Thy Spir - it? Or whither shall I flee from Thy
173
ppp Più lento. ♩= 72.
pp
pre - sence? If I say, Per-ad-venture the dark - - ness shall
174
poco animato.
f
co - ver me, Then shall my night be turned to day;
poco animato. ♩= 80.
cantabile

agitato e stringendo
Yea, the darkness is no darkness with Thee, But the
stringendo
night is as clear, clear as the day.
dim.
Tempo primo. ♩ = 72.
175
Sheol is naked before Thee, And Abaddon hath no
dim.
covering.
THE SINGERS.
CHORUS (remote.)
Blessed is the man whom Thou chastenest, That Thou may'st
poco

176
JUDAS.
"Rest from the days of ad-
p dolce
poco
ppp
give him rest from the days of ad-ver-si - ty.
give him rest from the days of ad-ver-si - ty.
give him rest from the days of ad-ver-si - ty.
give him rest from the days of ad-ver-si - ty.
176
ppp colla parte
Allegretto.
Quasi Recit.
molto espress.
mf
pp
A
-ver - si-ty."
Ne-ver man spake like this Man; He sa-tis-fi-ed the
Allegretto.
colla parte
R
a tempo
cantabile
177
long-ing soul, And fill - ed the hun-gry soul with good - -

accel.
- - ness.
CHORUS.
p cresc.
f accel.
—un - - til the pit be dig-ged for the wick-ed.
—un - - til the pit be dig-ged for the wick-ed.
—un - - til the pit be dig-ged for the wick-ed.
—un - - til the pit be dig-ged for the wick-ed.
accel.
sf
ff
178
Allegro molto.
JUDAS.
f disperato
Our life is short and
Allegro molto. ♩ = 126.
p fz
p sf
te-di-ous, and in the death of a man there is no rem-e-dy;

rf
L
nei - ther — was there an-y man known to have returned from the
colla parte
sf
179
parlando
grave. For we are born at all ad - ven-ture, and we shall
a tempo
ff
p
rit.
180 Poco meno mosso.
be hereafter as though we had never been: for the breath in our
Poco meno mosso.
ppp
nos - trils is as smoke, and a lit-tle spark in the

pp
181
mf
moving of our heart, Which being extinguished
pp
f
pp
our body shall be turned into ashes, and our
dim.
dim.
ppp
dim.
182
a tempo
p
spirit shall vanish as the soft air, And our
a tempo
ppp
cresc.
3
name shall be forgotten in time, and no man have our work in re-
sf

p
dolce
-mem-brance, and our life shall pass a-way as the
mf
f
dim.
183
pb
mf
trace of a cloud, and shall be dis-pers-ed as a
allargando
a tempo
pp
mist, that is driven away with the beams of the sun, and o-ver-
pp
dim.
dim. molto
184
R
Poco più lento.
-come with the heat there-of.
pp
The Lord know-eth the thoughts of
THE SINGERS, (within the Temple)
The Lord know-eth the thoughts of
The Lord know-eth the thoughts of
The Lord know-eth the thoughts of
CHORUS.
ppp
colla parte
Poco più lento. ♩= 72.

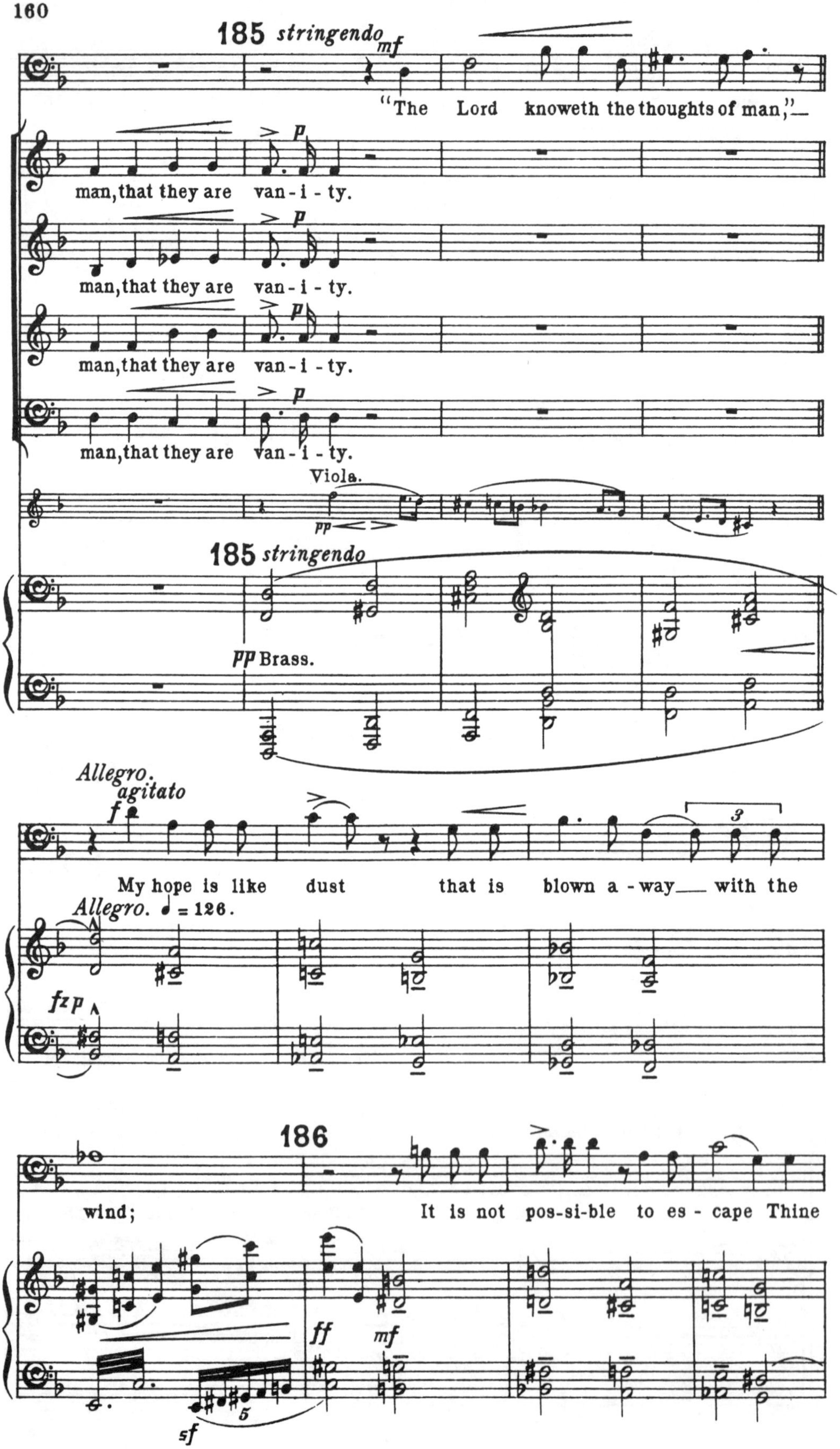

185 *stringendo* *mf*

"The Lord knoweth the thoughts of man,"—

man, that they are van-i-ty.

man, that they are van-i-ty.

man, that they are van-i-ty.

man, that they are van-i-ty.

Viola.

pp

185 *stringendo*

pp Brass.

Allegro. agitato

f

My hope is like dust that is blown a-way— with the

Allegro. ♩ = 126.

fz p

cresc.
hand; A sudden fear, and not look'd for, —
CHORUS.
Soprano.
THE PEOPLE.
(remote)
Alto.
Tenor.
Bass.
Cru-ci-fy Him!
Cru - ci - fy Him!
187
a tempo
comes upon me. —
They
cresc.
Cru -
(falsetto)
Cru-ci-fy Him!
a tempo

M

ff espress.
gather themselves toge - ther,
and con-
- ci - fy
Him!
- ci - fy
Him!
- ci - fy
Him!
- ci - fy
Him!
ff
p
cresc.
sf
p
cresc.
sf
ff
ff
- demn the in-nocent blood.
rf

188 ff disperato
stringendo
They con - demn the innocent blood.
fff feroce
Cru-ci-fy Him! Cru-ci-fy Him! Cru-ci-fy Him!
Cru-ci-fy Him! Cru-ci-fy Him! stringendo. Cru-ci-fy Him!
Cru-ci-fy Him! Cru - ci - fy Him! Cru-ci-fy Him!
Cru - ci-fy Him! Cru-ci-fy Him!
188
ff
stringendo.
Presto.
189 Andante.
f
Mine end is
♩=72.
Andante.
fz
p
sf
ffzpp
ff
p
cresc.
come, the mea-sure of my co-vet-ous-ness; O - ver
Vl. & Viola.
espress.
pp Brass.

190
mf
me is spread an heav - - y night, an im - age
Wood Wind.
sonoramente
pp con terrore
A
ad lib.
of that dark-ness which shall af-terward re -
ppp
pp
- ceive me: yet am I un - to my -
f
p
- self more griev - ous, more grievous than the
ff
rit.
sf
colla parte
sfp dim.
Ped.

191

f > *dim.* *Allegro.*

darkness.

Allegro. ♩ = 126.

pp

L *a tempo* *lunga.*

ff *cresc.* *fffz* *ppp* *sf*

192 *Andante.*

THE SINGERS, *(within the Temple)*

CHORUS.

ppp

He shall bring up-on them their own in - i - qui-ty.

He shall bring up-on them their own in - i - qui-ty.

He shall bring up-on them their own in - i - qui-ty.

192 *Andante.* ♩ = 69.

ppp *p*

V.
GOLGOTHA.

"E - li, E - li, la - ma sabach-tha - ni?"
Adagio. ♩ = 54.
con molto espress.
pp
cresc.
ppp lunga
trem.
ff
193
a tempo
CHORUS.
Soprano.
Alto.
Tenor.
Bass.
ppp
pppp
Tru - ly this was the Son of God.
Andante.
Andante. ♩ = 63.
MARY.
194
p
The sword hath pierc - ed through mine own soul.
molto espress.
Vl.
Horns p
pp

195
JOHN.
A
p
L
dim.
Thou hast trodden the wine - press a - lone,
p
MARY.
, ad lib.
pp
and of Thy peo - ple there was none, none with Thee.
p
L
colla parte
196
JOHN.
p
They shall look up - on Him Whom they have
Ped.
Ped.
MARY.
Recit.
p
as one mourneth for his
L
pp
pierced, and they shall mourn for Him,
pp
pp colla parte

a tempo
on - - ly son,
L
JOHN.
and shall be in bitterness for Him;
a tempo
197 MARY. Recit.
as one that is in bit - ter - ness for his first -
pp colla parte
- born.
198
The sword hath
a tempo, come prima.
A
L
Horns
L
molto espress.
pierc - ed through mine own soul.
f dim molto
pp colla parte
pp rit.

VI.

AT THE SEPULCHRE.

p
And they en-tered in, and found not the bo-dy of the
pp
Lord Je - - sus.
pp
is now a - blaze with light; The
pp
is now a - blaze with light; The
201
cresc.
rit.
p a tempo
dawn reacheth e-ven un-to He - - - - bron.
cresc.
p
dawn reacheth e-ven un-to He - - - - bron.
201
rit.
a tempo
Shofar.
colla parte
p

ANGELS.

SEMI-CHORUS.*

Poco più lento.

Soprano I.

p pp

Al - - - le - lu - - ia, —

Soprano II.

p pp

Al - - - - - le - lu - ia, —

Contralto I.

pp

Al - le - lu - - ia,

Contralto II.

p pp

Al - - - - - - - - - le - lu - - ia,

L - - - - - - - - - -

Poco più lento.

p dim. Voices. p

a tempo

R - - - - - - - - - - -

Al - - le - lu - - - -

Al - - - le - lu - - - -

a tempo

R - - - - - - - - - -

Al - - le - lu - - - -

Al - - le - lu - - - -

A a tempo - - - - - R - - - - - - - - - - -

dolce dim.

* Six voices only to each part.

202 Allegretto.
- ia!
- ia!
- ia!
ia!
202 Allegretto. ♩ = 104.
mf semplice
TUTTI.
mf semplice
dim.
S.
Why seek ye the liv - ing a-mong the dead?
C.
mf
203
p
TUTTI.
He is not here,
p semplice
cresc.
He is not here,
but is
203
p
cresc.

p cresc.
mf
but is ris - en, but is ris - en,
mf
p
ris - en, but is ris - en. Be - hold
p
204
R
mf a tempo
dim.
He is not here, but is
the place where they laid Him.
R
204
a tempo
pp
pp
L
f a tempo
dim.
ris - en. Go, tell His dis - ci - ples and
p
L
He is not here.
L
a tempo
pp
mf

p
Pe - ter that He go - eth be - fore you in - to
Go, tell His dis - ci - ples that He go - eth be - fore you in - to
pp
205
L
mf
Ga - li - lee. There shall ye see Him, there shall ye
Ga - li - lee. There shall ye see Him, there shall ye
206
dim.
p
see Him, as He said un - to you.
see Him, as He said.
He is not
dim.
R
pp
He is ris - en.
here; He is ris - en.

Poco più lento.
207
Semi-Chorus.
Soprano I.
Tutti.
cresc.
dim.
Più lento.
Semi-Chorus.
Al - le - lu - ia, Al - le - lu - - ia, Al - le -
Semi-Chorus.
Soprano II.
Tutti.
cresc.
dim.
Semi-Chorus.
Al - le - - lu - ia, Al - - le - lu - ia, Al - - le -
Semi-Chorus.
Contralto I.
Tutti.
cresc.
dim.
Semi-Chorus.
Al - le - lu - ia, Al - - le - lu - - ia, Al - le -
Semi-Chorus.
Contralto II.
Tutti.
cresc.
dim.
Semi-Chorus.
Al - le - lu - ia, Al - le - lu - - ia, Al - - le -
CHORUS.
207
Poco più lento.
Più lento.
Voices.
cresc.
dim.
- lu - - ia!
- lu - - ia!
- lu - - ia!
- lu - - ia!
molto rit.
dim.

VII.

THE ASCENSION.

209 Più lento.
JESUS. p dolce
Peace be un-to you.
Lento. p
Be-hold, I
Più lento. (♪ = ♩ of previous bar)
Lento. ♩ = 56.
pp
ppp
send the prom-ise of My Fa-ther up-on you:
Recit. pp
but tar-ry ye in the ci-ty of Je-ru-sa-lem,
a tempo
cresc.
un-
colla parte
a tempo
-til ye be en-du-ed with power from on high.
molto cresc.

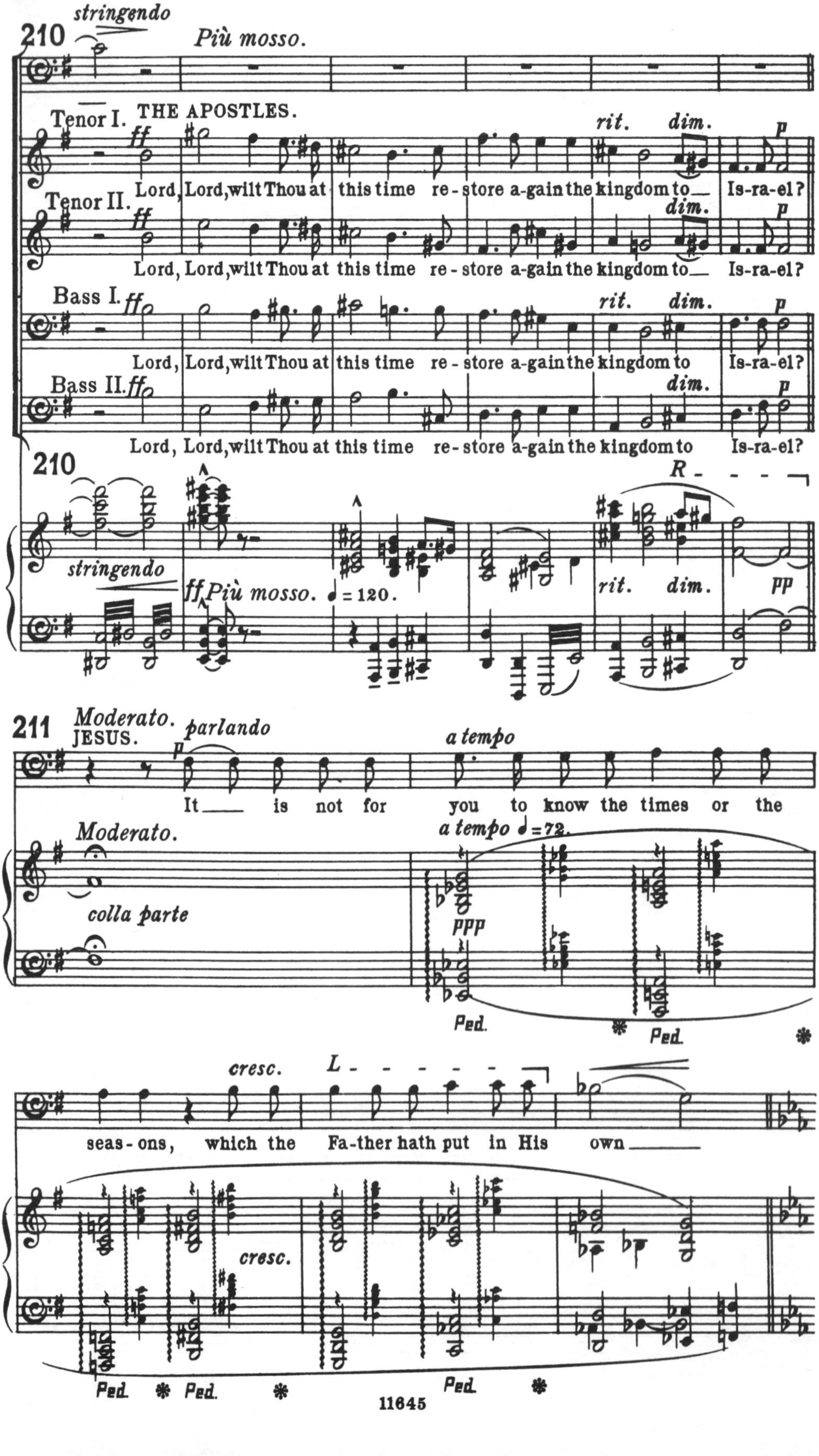

210
stringendo
Più mosso.
Tenor I. THE APOSTLES.
ff
rit. dim.
p
Lord, Lord, wilt Thou at this time re-store a-gain the kingdom to Is-ra-el?
Tenor II.
ff
dim.
p
Lord, Lord, wilt Thou at this time re-store a-gain the kingdom to Is-ra-el?
Bass I.
ff
rit. dim.
p
Lord, Lord, wilt Thou at this time re-store a-gain the kingdom to Is-ra-el?
Bass II.
ff
dim.
p
Lord, Lord, wilt Thou at this time re-store a-gain the kingdom to Is-ra-el?
210
R
stringendo
ff Più mosso. ♩= 120.
rit. dim.
pp
211
Moderato.
JESUS.
parlando
p
a tempo
It is not for you to know the times or the
Moderato.
colla parte
a tempo ♩= 72.
ppp
Ped.
Ped.
cresc.
L
seas-ons, which the Fa-ther hath put in His own
cresc.
Ped. Ped. Ped.

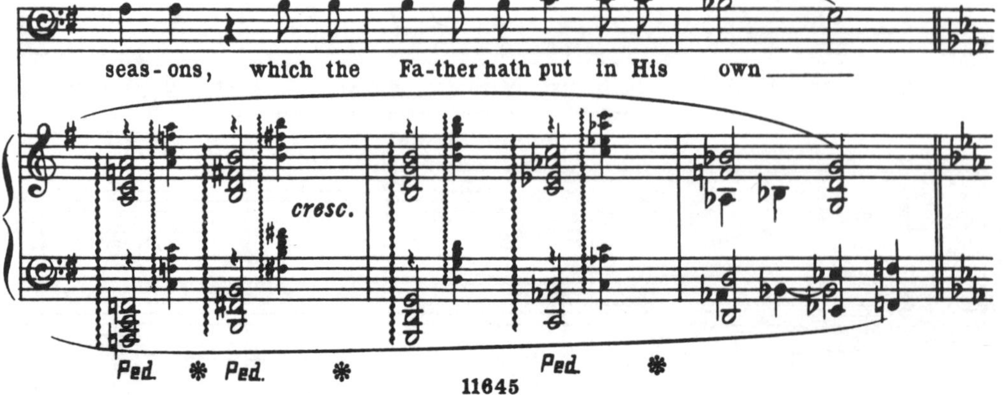

212
Più mosso.
animato
power. But ye shall re - ceive power, when the
Ho - ly Ghost is come up-on you.
rit.
213
molto largamente.
Go ye there-fore and teach all
molto largamente. ♪=96.
accel.
a tempo
dim.
Più lento.
solenne
na - tions, bap-tiz - ing them in the name of the Fa - ther,
a tempo ♩=66.
p accel.
pp colla parte

L
tranquillo
dolce
espress. rit.
pp
and of the Son, and of the Ho - ly Ghost:
L
dolce
tranquillo
ppp colla parte
214
a tempo
f
And, lo, I am with you,
a tempo ♩= 92.
f
p
mf
L'istesso tempo.
dim.
with you al - - - way, ev - en
L'istesso tempo.
p
pp
R
p
dim.
215
Andante.
un - to the end of the world.
Andante. ♩= 72.
colla parte
dim.
pp
ff

CONTRALTO.
Quasi Recit.
a tempo. Andante.
And when He had spok-en these things, while He
pp
216 L'istesso tempo.
blessed them—He was tak-en up; and a
dolcissimo
cloud re-ceiv-ed Him out of their sight;
and they look-ed sted-fast-ly to-ward

217
IN HEAVEN.
SEMI-CHORUS.
Soprano. L'istesso tempo.
Contralto.
CHORUS.
Soprano.
Contralto.
pp
Al - - le -
217
ON EARTH.
SOLI.
MARY.
Heav - - - en.
JOHN.
PETER.
CHORUS.
THE APOSTLES.
Tenor. legato
pp
Give us one heart, and one way: In Thy light shall
Bass I. pp legato
Give us one heart, and one way: In Thy light shall
217
8
L'istesso tempo.

pp
Al - - le - lu - - ia!
pp
Al - - -le - lu - - - -
- lu - ia!
espress.
mf
Give
MARY MAGDALENE.
espress.
mf
Give
espress.
mf
Give
espress.
mf
Give
we see light; Thou wilt shew us the path of
we see light; Thou wilt shew us the path of
espress.

218
- ia!
218
— us one — heart; —
us one heart;
us one heart, Give — us — one —
us one heart;
Give — us — one —
life.
Give us one
Bass I & II.
life.
Give us one
218
espress.

p
Al - - le - lu - - ia!
p
Al - - le - lu - - - ia!
p
My soul doth mag - ni - fy the Lord, And my
mf
Thou drew - est near in the
heart, and one way.
p legato
In Thy light shall we see light; Give us one heart, and one
heart, and one way.
heart.
legato
heart, In Thy light shall we see light; Give us one heart, and one

219
f
Al - -le lu - - - - - -ia!
Al - -le- -lu- - - -ia! Al - le-
pp
Al - -le - lu - - - - - - -ia! Al - le-
219
spir-it hath re-joiced in God my Sa - - -viour.
dim.
day that I call-ed up - on Thee: Thou saidst, Fear not.
espress. cantabile
p
way. For He hath not des-
way.
219
L.H.

Al - le-lu - ia!
Al - le-lu - ia!
Al - le-lu - ia!
Al - le-lu - ia!
- lu - - ia!
Al - le - lu - - ia!
- lu - - ia!
Al - le - lu - - ia!
espress.
Nei-ther
- pis - ed nor ab - hor - red the af - flic - tion of the af -
Nei-ther hath He hid His

f
dim.
hath He hid His face from him; But when he
p
f
dim.
Nei - ther hid His face from him; But when he
mf
f
dim.
Nei-ther hid His face from him; But when
f
dim.
-flict-ed; Nei - ther hid His face from him; But when
p
f
dim.
Nei-ther hid His face from him; But when he
f
dim.
face, nei-ther hid His face from him; But when
f
dim.

220
p
Al - le - lu - - ia!
p
Al - le - lu - - ia!
espress.
p
220
cri - ed un - to Him, He heard.
p
cri - - ed un - to Him, He heard.
espress.
p
he cri - ed un - to Him, He heard.
p
he cri - ed un - to Him, He heard.
espress.
p
cri - ed un - to Him, He heard.
p
legato
p
he cri - ed un - to Him, He heard. All the ends of the
220

221 Mistico
p
pp
Al - - le - lu - ia!
"Ho - ly Fa - ther,
Al - - le - lu - ia!
"Ho - ly Fa - ther,
Mistico
"Ho - ly Fa - ther,
"Ho - - ly
221
pp molto legato
All the ends of the
All the ends of the
All the ends of the
All the ends of the
ppp
And all the
world shall re - mem - ber and turn un - to the Lord. And all the
221
Ped. * Ped. *

cresc.
keep through Thine own name those whom Thou hast
keep through Thine own name those whom Thou hast
keep through Thine own name those whom Thou hast
Fa - - ther keep those whom Thou hast given Me,
world shall re - mem - - ber and turn un - to the Lord: And all the
world shall re - mem - - ber and turn un - to the Lord: And all the
world shall re - mem - - ber and turn un - to the Lord: And all the
world shall re - mem - - ber and turn un - to the Lord: And all the
kin - - dreds of the na - - tions shall
kin - - dreds of the na - - - tions shall
Ped. Ped. Ped. Ped. Ped. Ped.

222
f dim.
giv - en Me, that they may be one, as We are."
giv - en Me, that they may be one, as We are."
giv - en Me, that they may be one, as We are."
that they may be one, as We are."
222
kin - dreds of the nations shall wor - ship be-fore Thee.
kin - dreds of the nations shall wor - ship be-fore Thee.
kin - dreds of the nations shall wor - ship be-fore Thee.
kin - dreds of the nations shall wor - ship be-fore Thee.
f ff
wor - ship, wor - ship be - fore Thee. For the
wor - ship, wor - ship be - fore Thee. For the
222
ff
Ped. * Ped. * Ped. * Ped. *

p ff dim. pp
Al-le-lu-ia!
dim. pp ppp
For the kingdom is the Lord's: And He is the governor a-mong the
f dim. p
king-dom is the Lord's: And He is the governor a-mong the
dim.

223
Poco meno mosso.
mistico
ppp
dim.
"I have done Thy com-mand-ment,
"I have done Thy com-mand-ment,
223
Poco meno mosso.
nations.
nations.
nations.
nations.
pp
ppp
na-tions.
"In the world ye shall
na-tions.
"In the world ye shall
223 Poco meno mosso.
pp

SEMI-CHORUS.
CHORUS.
dim.
I have fin - ished the work which Thou
dim.
I have fin - ished the work which Thou
ppp
have trib - - u - la - - tion: But
ppp
have trib - - u - la - - tion: But
molto
ga - vest Me to do;
I laid down My
molto
ga - vest Me to do;
I laid down My
224
be of good cheer,
be of good cheer,
224

225
life for the sheep."
life for the sheep."
parlando
ppp
"What are these wounds in Thine
ppp
"What are these wounds in Thine
ppp
I have ov - er-come the world."
ppp
I have ov - er-come the world."
225
225
ppp
SEMI-CHORUS.
pp
"Those with which I was wounded in the house of My
pp
"Those with which I was wounded in the house of My
CHORUS.
hands?"
hands?"
colla parte

226
friends."
friends."
pp
They plat-ted a crown of thorns, And
pp
They plat-ted a crown of thorns, And
226
pp
put it a-bout His head,— They mock-ed Him, They spat up-on Him, They
dim.
put it a-bout His head,— They mock-ed Him, They spat up-on Him, They
dim.
pp

227
rit.
a tempo
228
Al - le - lu - ia!
Al - le - lu - ia! Al - le - lu - ia!
smote Him with a reed, — They cru - ci - fied Him.
smote Him with a reed, — They cru - ci - fied Him.
rit.
ppp
pp
229
Al - le - lu - ia! Al - le - lu - ia!
Al - le - lu - ia! Al - le - lu - ia!
CHORUS.
Tenor.
Bass.
Give us
Give
Trombe.
Ped.

SEMI-CHORUS.
CHORUS.
SOLI.
sostenuto
p
They shall come, and shall de-
sostenuto
p
They shall come, and shall de-
CHORUS.
one heart, and one way; In Thy light
us one heart, In Thy light
us one heart, In Thy light
Celli etc:
Trombe.
Celli etc:
8

230

p "Now I am

p "Now I am

p "Now I am

p "Now I am

sostenuto p

They shall come and de - clare His right - eous - ness

- clare His right - eous - ness,

p sostenuto

They shall come and de - clare His right-eous - ness

- clare His right - eous - ness,

shall we see light. f Give us one

shall we see light. f Give us one

230

f mf L.H.

no more in the world, But these
no more in the world, But these
no more in the world, But these
no more in the world, But these
cantabile
un - - to a peo - ple that
cantabile
They shall de - clare, they shall de-
cantabile
un - - to a peo - ple that
cantabile
They shall de - clare, they shall de-
heart, Give us one way.
heart, Give us one way.

* The time must be increased until the last bar before the Andante; this must equal 𝅗𝅥 = 84.

mf
They shall
mf
They shall
mf
They shall
He is the gov-ern-or a - mong the
rf
rf
Lord's, the king - dom is the Lord's:
(𝅗𝅥 = 84)
sf
sf
sf

*These triplets should be equal to the last triplet of crotchets in the previous bar.

233 Più lento.
molto sostenuto
tutta forza
fff
From hence - - forth shall the
From hence - - forth shall the
From hence - - forth shall the
From hence - - forth shall the
hath done this. They
hath done this. They
hath done this. They
done this. They
All the ends of the world shall re - mem -
All the ends of the world shall re - mem -
233 Più lento. ♩ = 60.
Ped.

largamente
Son of man be seat - - ed
Son of man be seat - - ed
largamente
Son of man be seat - - ed
Son of man be seat - - -
shall declare His right - eous-ness.
shall declare His right - eous-ness.
largamente
shall declare His right - eous-ness Un-to a peo - ple that
shall declare His right - eous-ness.
largamente
- - - ber and turn un - to the Lord: And all the kin - dreds
- - ber and turn un - to the Lord: And all the kin - dreds
largamente
Ped. * Ped. * Ped. * Ped. * Ped. *

ffz
at the right hand of the
ffz
at the right hand of the
ffz
at the right hand of the
ffz
-ed at the right hand of the
ffz
That He hath
ff
That He hath done
ffz
shall be born, that He, that He hath done this.
ff
That He hath done
ffz
of the na - tions shall wor - ship be - fore
ffz
of the na - tions shall wor - ship be - fore
ffz
Ped.
Ped.
Ped.
Ped.
Ped.

Nobilmente
L
234
dim.
rf
power of God.
power of God.
power of God.
power of God. Al - le-lu - - - - ia!
234
done, that He
this. They shall come and shall declare the right - - eousness Un-to a
They shall de-clare, shall declare that
this. They shall de-clare that He hath done this, that He
Thee, wor - - - - - - - ship, the
na - - - tions shall
Thee, All the kin - dreds of the na - - - tions shall
234 Nobilmente
sostenuto
tutta forza

Al - - le
Al - - le-
Al - - le - lu - - ia!
Al - - le-lu - ia!
Al - - le - lu - - - ia! Al - le - lu - - - ia! Al - le-
hath done this.
peo-ple that shall be born that He hath done this.
He hath done this. Al - le - lu - ia!
hath done this. Al - le - lu - ia!
kin - dreds of the na - - tions shall wor-ship, shall wor-ship be-fore
wor - - ship, shall wor - - - - ship be-
dim.

235
dim.
p
- lu - ia!
Al - le -
- lu - - - ia!
Al - le - lu - ia!
- lu - - - ia!
Al - le - lu - - - ia!
Thee.
- fore
Thee.
dim.
pp

-lu - - ia! Al-le-
-lu - - ia! Al-le-
-lu - - ia! Al-le-
-lu - - ia! Al-le-
-lu - - ia! Al-le-
-lu - - ia! Al-le-
arpegg. simile

236
p
-lu - - - ia!
Al - le -
-lu - - - ia!
p
-lu - - - ia!
Al - le -
-lu - - - ia!
cantabile ed espress.
236
p molto cresc.
In His love and in His
p molto cresc.
In His love and in His
p molto cresc.
In His love and in His
p molto cresc.
In His love and in His
p
-lu - - - ia!
Al - le -
-lu - - - ia!
236
8
sonoramente

pp
-lu - - - - ia! Al - le - lu - -
p
pp
Al - le - lu - ia! Al - - le - lu - ia! Al - le -
pp
-lu - - - - ia! Al - le - lu - -
p
pp
Al - le - lu - ia! Al - - le - lu - ia! Al - le -
f
p
pi - ty He re - deem - ed them.
f
p
pi - ty He re - deem - ed them.
f
p
pi - ty He re - deem - ed them.
f
p
pi - ty He re - deem - ed them.
pp
- lu - ia! Al - le - lu - ia! Al - le -
p
Al - le - lu - ia! Al - le - lu - ia! Al - le - lu -
3
3
morendo

Printed and bound in Great Britain by
Caligraving Limited Thetford Norfolk

9/02 (45325)

CHORAL WORKS FOR MIXED VOICES

ach	**Christmas Oratorio** for soprano, alto, tenor & bass soli, SATB & orchestra
	Mass in B minor for two sopranos, alto, tenor & bass soli, SSATB & orchestra
	St Matthew Passion for soprano, alto, tenor & bass soli, SATB & orchestra
rahms	**Requiem** for soprano & baritone soli, SATB & orchestra
lgar	**Give unto the Lord Psalm 29** for SATB & organ or orchestra
auré	**Requiem** for soprano & baritone soli, SATB & orchestra *edited by Desmond Ratcliffe*
andel	**Messiah** for soprano, alto, tenor & bass soli, SATB & orchestra *edited by Watkins Shaw*
aydn	**Creation** for soprano, tenor & bass soli, SATB & orchestra
	Imperial 'Nelson' Mass for soprano, alto, tenor & bass soli, SATB & orchestra
	Maria Theresa Mass for soprano, alto, tenor & bass soli, SATB & orchestra
	Mass in time of War 'Paukenmesse' for soprano, alto, tenor & bass soli, SATB & orchestra
onteverdi	**Beatus Vir** for soloists, double choir, organ & orchestra *edited by Denis Stevens & John Steele*
	Magnificat for SSATB chorus, instruments & organ *edited by John Steele*
	Vespers for soloists, double choir, organ & orchestra *edited by Denis Stevens*
ozart	**Requiem Mass** for soprano, alto, tenor & bass soli, SATB & orchestra
carlatti	**Dixit Dominus** for SATB, soli & chorus, string orchestra & organ continuo *edited by John Steele*

33)

The Choral Music of Edward Elgar

Apostles, The
oratorio for SATBB soli, chorus & orchestra

Caractacus
cantata for STBar soli, chorus & orchestra

Dream of Gerontius, The
oratorio for M-S TB soli, chorus & orchestra

Early Part Songs, The (1890 – 1891)

Five Unaccompanied Part-Songs opus 71, 72 & 73

Four Unaccompanied Part-Songs opus 53

From the Greek Anthology
five unaccompanied part-songs for TTBB

Give Unto the Lord (Psalm 29)
for chorus & orchestra

Kingdom, The
oratorio for SATB soli, chorus & orchestra

Later Part-Songs, The (1902 – 1925)

Light of Life, The (Lux Christi)
oratorio for SATBar soli, chorus & orchestra

Music Makers, The
ode for Contralto solo, chorus & orchestra

Seven Anthems

Spirit of England, The
for S or T solo, chorus & orchestra

Three Unaccompanied Part-Songs

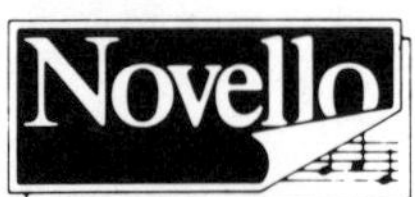

302(83)